Communications in Computer and Information Science   2923

Series Editors

Gang Li , *School of Information Technology, Deakin University, Burwood, VIC, Australia*

Joaquim Filipe, *Polytechnic Institute of Setúbal, Setúbal, Portugal*

Zhiwei Xu, *Chinese Academy of Sciences, Beijing, China*

Rationale

The CCIS series is devoted to the publication of proceedings of computer science conferences. Its aim is to efficiently disseminate original research results in informatics in printed and electronic form. While the focus is on publication of peer-reviewed full papers presenting mature work, inclusion of reviewed short papers reporting on work in progress is welcome, too. Besides globally relevant meetings with internationally representative program committees guaranteeing a strict peer-reviewing and paper selection process, conferences run by societies or of high regional or national relevance are also considered for publication.

Topics

The topical scope of CCIS spans the entire spectrum of informatics ranging from foundational topics in the theory of computing to information and communications science and technology and a broad variety of interdisciplinary application fields.

Information for Volume Editors and Authors

Publication in CCIS is free of charge. No royalties are paid, however, we offer registered conference participants temporary free access to the online version of the conference proceedings on SpringerLink (http://link.springer.com) by means of an http referrer from the conference website and/or a number of complimentary printed copies, as specified in the official acceptance email of the event.

CCIS proceedings can be published in time for distribution at conferences or as post-proceedings, and delivered in the form of printed books and/or electronically as USBs and/or e-content licenses for accessing proceedings at SpringerLink. Furthermore, CCIS proceedings are included in the CCIS electronic book series hosted in the SpringerLink digital library at http://link.springer.com/bookseries/7899. Conferences publishing in CCIS are allowed to use our online conference service (Meteor) for managing the whole proceedings lifecycle (from submission and reviewing to preparing for publication) free of charge.

Publication process

The language of publication is exclusively English. Authors publishing in CCIS have to sign the Springer CCIS copyright transfer form, however, they are free to use their material published in CCIS for substantially changed, more elaborate subsequent publications elsewhere. For the preparation of the camera-ready papers/files, authors have to strictly adhere to the Springer CCIS Authors' Instructions and are strongly encouraged to use the CCIS LaTeX style files or templates.

Abstracting/Indexing

CCIS is abstracted/indexed in DBLP, Google Scholar, EI-Compendex, Mathematical Reviews, SCImago, Scopus. CCIS volumes are also submitted for the inclusion in ISI Proceedings.

How to start

To start the evaluation of your proposal for inclusion in the CCIS series, please send an e-mail to ccis@springer.com

Yazan Mualla · Liuwen Yu · Hui Zhao ·
Amro Najjar · Davide Liga
Editors

Advances in Explainable Agentic AI and Large Language Models

Second International Workshop, CALM 2025
Luxembourg City, Luxembourg, December 1-5, 2025
Proceedings

 Springer

Editors
Yazan Mualla
Université de Technologie de
Belfort-Montbéliard
Belfort Cedex, France

Hui Zhao
Tongji University
Shanghai, China

Davide Liga
University of Luxembourg
Esch-sur-Alzette, Luxembourg

Liuwen Yu
Luxembourg Institute of Science
and Technology
Belval, Luxembourg

Amro Najjar
Luxembourg Institute of Science
and Technology
Belval, Luxembourg

ISSN 1865-0929   ISSN 1865-0937 (electronic)
Communications in Computer and Information Science
ISBN 978-3-032-20547-6   ISBN 978-3-032-20548-3 (eBook)
https://doi.org/10.1007/978-3-032-20548-3

This Springer imprint is published by the registered company Springer Nature Switzerland AG
The registered company address is: Gewerbestrasse 11, 6330 Cham, Switzerland

If disposing of this product, please recycle the paper.

Preface

The Workshop on Causality, Agents, and Large Models (CALM) fosters interdisciplinary collaboration at the intersection of causal reasoning, multi-agent systems (MAS), and large language models (LLMs). These areas jointly shape how AI systems reason, coordinate, and adapt in complex environments. CALM provides a forum to develop foundations, address technical challenges, and identify emerging research directions.

CALM 2025 was held in Luxembourg from 1–5 December 2025, in conjunction with the Luxembourg Logic & AI Summit.

We received 15 submissions from institutions across Europe and beyond, including the US, the UK, France, Spain, Luxembourg, and Poland.

All papers underwent double-blind peer review, each evaluated by at least 3 reviewers. We enforced strict conflict-of-interest procedures; submissions co-authored by program committee members were properly considered to ensure independent reviewing.

The program committee selected 8 full papers for presentation and inclusion in these proceedings. The accepted contributions span different topic clusters, including agentic automation, causation, and large models, highlighting both methodological advances and real-world applications.

The research presented at CALM 2025 reflected a push toward integrating structural causal models with the scaled reasoning capabilities of LLMs. A primary research direction involved the transition from statistical association to interventionist reasoning, where agents use formal logics to decompose multi-agent behaviors and attribute responsibility within complex workflows. Contributors explored new heuristics for model–data alignment to ensure that neural architectures accurately reflect the underlying causal structures of their training sets. Furthermore, the workshop highlighted advances in decentralized coordination and hybrid metaheuristic frameworks, demonstrating how reinforcement learning can be leveraged for explainable artificial intelligence (XAI) in high-stakes environments.

The concept of explainable agentic AI emerged as a cornerstone of the workshop, marking a shift from passive language generation toward autonomous systems that perform multi-step actions while remaining transparent to humans. This "agentification" was exemplified by the development of Large Action Models (LAMs), which augmented traditional tutor agents with multimodal interaction capabilities. Significant attention was focused on the supervision of physical agents, such as autonomous tractors and social robots. These systems aimed to demystify complex behaviors by providing natural language justifications and auditable decision traces, ensuring that proactive, goal-driven agents remain aligned with human-centered safety and accountability standards

We thank the authors for their submissions, the reviewers and program committee for their careful and timely work, and our invited speakers for enriching the workshop with their perspectives. We hope this volume stimulates further research and collaboration on building AI systems that are both effective and responsible.

January 2026

Yazan Mualla
Liuwen Yu
Davide Liga
Amro Najjar
Hui Zhao

Organization

General Chair

Yazan Mualla	Université de Technologie de Belfort-Montbéliard, France

Program Committee Chairs

Davide Liga	University of Luxembourg, Luxembourg
Yazan Mualla	Université de Technologie de Belfort-Montbéliard France
Amro Najjar	Luxembourg Institute of Science and Technology Luxembourg
Liuwen Yu	Luxembourg Institute of Science and Technology, Luxembourg
Hui Zhao	Tongji University, China

Steering Committee

Stéphane Galland	Université de Technologie de Belfort-Montbéliard, France
Abdeljalil Abbas-Turki	Université de Technologie de Belfort-Montbéliard, France

Program Committee

Adeel Ahmad	Université du Littoral Côte d'Opale, France
Ilaria Angela Amantea	Università di Torino, Italy
Sukriti Bhattacharya	Luxembourg Institute of Science and Technology, Luxembourg
Shiva Kumar Bhuram	Dorman Products, USA
Badreddine Chah	Université de Technologie Belfort-Montbéliard, France
Alaa Daoud	Université Polytechnique de Hauts de France, France

Fatima-Zahrae El-Qoraychy	Université de Technologie Belfort-Montbéliard, France
Wachara Fungwacharakorn	National Institute of Informatics, Japan
Stéphane Galland	Université de Technologie Belfort-Montbéliard, France
Federico Galli	University of Bologna, Italy
Syrine Haddad	Université de Technologie Belfort-Montbéliard, France
Nina Hosseini-Kivanani	University of Luxembourg, Luxembourg
Eskandar Kouicem	Snowflake, France
Yanming Liu	Zhejiang University, China
Alexandre Lombard	Université de Technologie Belfort-Montbéliard, France
Jeet Mehta	Netflix, USA
Utsav Patel	Independent Researcher, USA
Arianna Rossi	Sant'Anna School of Advanced Studies, Italy
Francesco Sovrano	Università della Svizzera italiana, Switzerland
Bianca Steffes	Saarland University, Germany
Hedi Tebourbi	University of Luxembourg, Luxembourg
Stefano Tedeschi	Università della Valle d'Aosta – Université de la Vallée d'Aoste, Italy
May Myo Zin	National Institute of Informatics, Japan

Additional Reviewers

Jiangchuan Gong	Kejian Tong
Xiaolan Ke	Yuanjing Zhu
Honggang Li	Yingying Zhuang
Yujian Long	

Contents

Towards A Human-Centered Approach to Supervision of Explainable Autonomous Robot Tractors

Syrine Haddad[1]($\boxtimes$) (ID), Moustafa Zouinar[2] (ID), Yazan Mualla[1] (ID), and Abdeljalil Abbas-Turki[1] (ID)

[1] University of Technology of Belfort-Montbeliard, UTBM, CIAD UR 7533, 90010 Belfort, France
{syrine.haddad,yazan.mualla,abdeljalil.abbas-turki}@utbm.fr
[2] Orange Innovation - SENSE & Le Cnam/CRTD, 92320 Châtillon, France
moustafa.zouinar@orange.com

Abstract. Industrial autonomous robot tractors are increasingly deployed in logistics yards for trailer transport and docking. Yet, most research and systems prioritize safety and automation performance, while overlooking the human aspects involved in supervising these tractors. This imbalance risks reducing efficiency and safety in practice. We argue that supervision of autonomous tractors must be recentered on the human aspects of logistics through Human-Computer Interaction, ergonomics, and Human-in-the-loop principles. Drawing on an activity analysis of workflows in a representative logistics hub, we identify critical tasks and propose three design considerations for a human-centered design of supervision systems of autonomous robot tractors. We outline a lightweight conceptual framework that embeds transparency, explainability, ergonomics, and trust calibration into supervisory interfaces. We believe that the autonomous robot tractors can only be safely and effectively integrated into logistics operations by reframing supervision as a human-centered issue.

Keywords: Human-Computer Interaction · Human-in-the-loop · Ergonomics · Logistics Automation · Explainability

1 Introduction

Autonomous robot tractors are increasingly being deployed in logistics centers and warehouse yards to automate tasks such as trailer transport, pallet movement, and docking operations. Although these systems are advanced in technology, they operate in dynamic contexts where complete autonomy is still fragile, necessitating efficient human supervision [8]. However, current supervisory frameworks often neglect principles from Human-Computer Interaction (HCI) and ergonomics, leading to unintuitive User Interfaces (UIs), high cognitive workload, and limited Situational Awareness (SA) [2,3].

Industrial research on autonomous tractors has primarily focused on safety, while ergonomics and usability have remained underexplored. This creates a gap

Y. Mualla et al. (Eds.): CALM 2025, CCIS 2923, pp. 1–12, 2026.
https://doi.org/10.1007/978-3-032-20548-3_1

between what robots can technically achieve and how operators can supervise them effectively. We argue for a shift toward human-centered supervision systems that treat operators not as passive monitors, but as active collaborators capable of handling anomalies and making safety-critical decisions. Field observations indicate that current 'black-box' autonomy often leads to operator mistrust and excessive manual interventions, which paradoxically reduce the efficiency gains of automation. By centering supervision on human needs, we aim to reduce these unnecessary interventions and improve overall system resilience. They also need to be able to understand the autonomous robot tractors' behaviors, which raises the issue of transparency/explainability. Autonomous tractors are based on Artificial Intelligence (AI) systems that process real-time data from multiple sensors and operate in unpredictable, changing conditions. However, modern autonomous vehicles rely on complex Machine Learning (ML) algorithms, which are opaque, raising transparency issues for humans, for example, when the vehicle makes an unexpected or incorrect decision or breaks down. Understanding these decisions can therefore be challenging [1]. We argue that this issue of transparency should be treated from a human-centered perspective that encompasses the human aspects of autonomous tractor supervision. Drawing on the activity-centered ergonomics approach [5], a particular feature of our approach is that the analysis of workers' activities and tasks is a crucial first step for identifying their needs in terms of transparency, and more globally, of supervision of the tractors.

This paper proposes a set of human-centered design principles drawn from the literature. Building on an activity-based analysis of warehouse workflows and field observations, we examine how these principles align with real supervisory practices and highlight opportunities to enhance transparency and incorporate eXplainable AI (XAI) in robotic tractor supervision. To the best of our knowledge, the proposed design framework for humanautonomous agent interaction is novel in explicitly linking supervision needs to UI requirements through a formal designactivity mapping. Prior studies have not integrated these elements in a unified framework, making our approach a unique contribution to the field.

The paper is organized as follows. First, we review related work on industrial autonomous robot systems, ergonomics, and supervisory interfaces, highlighting gaps in current approaches for logistics robots. Next, we propose a set of design guidelines for human-centered supervision, grounded in HCI and ergonomics principles. We then present an activity and workflow analysis of warehouse operations, focusing on the key roles and decision points that structure supervision needs, by interpreting how these guidelines could be applied to the observed activities, highlighting their potential applications and the challenges of real-world implementation. This is followed by a discussion that situates our contribution within ongoing research on supervision and ergonomics in logistics automation. Finally, we conclude by summarizing our paper and outlining directions for future work on transparent and effective supervisory systems for autonomous robot tractors.

2   Related Work

Our paper explores various research areas, including the role of humans in automated production environments, which is referred to as Human-in-the-loop (HITL) [7], XAI, autonomous robots, and the design and integration of autonomous systems in work environments. Currently, supervision of industrial mobile robots typically relies on 2D map visualizations or raw video feeds. These interfaces display the robot's location, but rarely reveal why it is there or what it intends to do next, forcing operators to infer its "intent". This gap is critical given safety standards like ISO 3691-4, which emphasize the need for clear signalling of automated vehicle "intent" to personnel in shared spaces. HITL is positioned as vital for achieving effective integration of autonomous systems in the evolving landscape of Industry 5.0 [7]. This concept has been developed in human factors to emphasize the important role of humans in production systems. It has been introduced following observations that showed that, when an operator is out of the loop, i.e., moved out of a control loop due to automated control, this situation impairs the operator's activity, by limiting their awareness of the system's states. This hinders their ability to maintain control of the systems and intervene in the event of breakdowns. Reframing supervision necessitates precise definitions of human control modes. Routine monitoring of autonomous tractor operations aligns with a Human-on-the-loop (HOTL) role, where the operator primarily serves as a passive observer. The supervisory interface's primary ergonomic mandate is to facilitate a seamless, high-awareness transition from HOTL monitoring to active HITL collaboration and control. Providing the human with appropriate and meaningful informational feedback regarding the behavior of autonomous systems is therefore crucial. This requirement leads to the issue of transparency and explainability, which have become important topics in robotics with the use of ML models [17]. The concept of transparency should thus be framed not merely as a description of algorithmic inputs, but as a mechanism for aligning the human operator's cognitive model with the agent's behavioral policy [23]. Alongside technical work, the human aspects of this issue become equally important. It raises several questions, for example: *What level of transparency is needed? Who will need transparency/explanations? How to design relevant and meaningful explanations? In which context and for which tasks are they required? How should transparent information be displayed?* Addressing these questions is crucial for designing effective and user-friendly transparency/explainability features in AI and robotics systems. The treatment of these questions requires the mobilization of human-computer principles developed in ergonomics and User Experience (UX), as well as a good understanding of the operators' actual or future activities and the organizational context in which the autonomous system will be introduced.

Prior work has highlighted the importance of ergonomics and user-centered approaches in industrial automation. For example, Fröhlich et al. [7] examine decision-making, control, and "collaboration" [16] between humans and computers, identifying challenges for HCI in creating safe, effective, and user-friendly production systems, while stressing the role of ergonomics in improving UX and safety. Similarly, Colceriu et al. [4] developed a user-centered graphical UI for mobile human-robot cooperation in industrial assembly, guided by ISO 9241 principles and evaluated through heuristic methods, usability testing, and SA measures, achieving high usability and transferability to contexts such as logistics. Complementing this, Simões et al. [22] provide a broad review of collaborative human-robot environments, arguing for multidisciplinary approaches that combine engineering, ergonomics, and psychology to promote safe, efficient, and human-centered workplaces. However, existing research does not systematically integrate workflow and activity analysis with ergonomic design principles to support the supervision of autonomous robotic tractors in logistics. In this paper, we argue that such integration is essential to re-frame tractor supervision from a purely technical challenge into a human-centered issue, and we propose a framework that builds on activity analysis to guide the design of ergonomic and transparent supervisory systems.

3   Towards a Framework for Human-Centered Supervision of Robotic Tractors

Supervising robotic tractors in dynamic logistics environments mandates interfaces that are usable and responsive to human needs, as well as transparent, the tractors' behaviors should be easily comprehensible to operators. Based on insights from HCI, Human-Robot Interaction (HRI), and ergonomics literature [4], we identify three key design considerations that can serve as the foundation of effective human-centered supervision systems.

3.1   Transparency and Situational Awareness

Interfaces should make the system state and future actions visible so operators can answer: *"What is the robot doing?"*, *"Why is it doing that?"*, and *"What does it intend to do next?"*. Techniques such as visual "intent" projections, real-time path previews, and activity logs support SA in dynamic yards [6,20]. This reflects Norman's principles of *visibility* and *feedback* [14], and Bastien and Scapin's *Immediate Feedback* criterion [19]. While conventional XAI methods (e.g., feature attribution or saliency-based explanations) can provide insight into perception or classification tasks, they are insufficient for sequential, goal-driven planning agents such as autonomous tractors. Supervisors require explanations that align the agent's internal plan and goal structure with human expectations, particularly when anomalies occur or actions deviate from anticipated trajectories. To align the agent's policy with the human's mental model, the proposed Causal XAI mechanism must be structural. For sequential, goal-driven planning agents (such as those based on a Behavior Tree (BT) architecture), explanations are not derived from static classification features but directly from the agent's internal decision logic. The Causal XAI process requires building a graphical model from the agent's policy structure and runtime memory to generate precise, temporal counterfactual explanations. This approach allows the interface to clarify not just *what* decision was made, but *why* that specific plan was chosen, given the current state and constraints, providing high-fidelity decision traceability. For a technical grounding of this approach, we draw on methods for generating temporal counterfactuals from BT states [11]. To sustain SA in dynamic logistics environments, it is important to provide operators with UIs that help them to perceive the robots and their movements, to understand and to anticipate their behaviors (e.g., for example in terms of trajectories). The understanding and projection features are clearly related to transparency and explainability issues [18].

3.2   Cognitive Workload Management

Supervisors may often monitor multiple vehicles simultaneously. This may increase cognitive load. To avoid this issue, it is crucial to design UIs that do not augment information density and that adapt to context (e.g., when several tractors are operating simultaneously, the UI could automatically highlight only the tractors that deviate from their planned paths or require human intervention, while minimizing the display of routine status information) and enable prioritization of tasks. Following Bastien and Scapin's *Workload* criterion, systems must minimize memory load, allowing operators to concentrate on critical decision-making tasks without distraction [19]. Regarding transparency, Mualla et al. [12] argued that parsimonious explanations and filtering unnecessary information enhance user understanding, reduce cognitive load, and facilitate smoother human-agent collaboration, ultimately improving operational efficiency and safety. Their proposed architecture, HAExA [13], operationalizes this principle by generating concise, contrastive explanations and adaptively filtering them according to cognitive load thresholds. Empirical validation showed that this approach improves trust and satisfaction, further supporting explanation filtering as a mechanism for effective workload management in supervisory interfaces.

3.3   Trust Calibration

Operators must neither over-trust nor under-trust autonomous behavior [9]. Interfaces should convey the system's confidence in its own perceptions and plans, highlight uncertain decisions, and present concise justifications for actions. All of this may help operators to calibrate their trust. Such features directly support Norman's principle of *Feedback*, since they provide operators with clear and timely information about the system's state, enabling them to adjust their cognitive models and intervention strategies accordingly [14]. In high-stakes logistics, misplaced trust can lead to either excessive intervention, such as slowing operations, or delayed reaction to faults. Progressive disclosure of information, for example, showing basic status at a glance and allowing drill-down for diagnostics, can help to calibrate trust without overwhelming users. Training scenarios and simulation-based previews of system limits can further strengthen appropriate reliance and operator confidence.

4   Advancing an Application of the Framework

To illustrate how the previously introduced human-centered design guidelines can guide practical system design for the supervision of robot tractors, we consider a representative mid-sized logistics hub on the outskirts of Paris, reflecting typical operations in European freight forwarding facilities. This site, which integrates yard management, trailer handling, and intermodal operations, is involved in a research project aiming at exploring and testing a robot tractor for trailer handling. This goal requires the development of a supervision system that will help human operators to supervise the robot. In this perspective, considering the human-centered and ergonomics approach, we started by analyzing how trailers are currently moved by human operators and how the movement of trailers is organized. This first step is crucial as it will help us to understand what the robot will have to do, what it will not be able to do, and what human operators will need in terms of supervision, including transparency.

4.1   Activity Analysis of Trailers Management

The analysis reveals the main stages of the process: trailer arrival and check-in, pallet movement, intra-yard navigation, and docking. These stages involve multiple human actors whose coordination ensures that trailers are managed efficiently and safely. Figure 1 presents a simplified sequence diagram for a possible scenario of trailer yard management, showing key actors and decision points. The primary roles can be described as follows:

- `Scheduler`: Initiates daily shipment data and requirements.
- `Transport Department`: Generates an initial transport plan based on incoming requests and operational constraints.
- `Logistics Clerk`: Verifies, adjusts, and refines the plan to align with yard capacity and scheduling logistics.
- `Yard-driver`: Coordinates yard activities, validates movement plans, manages dock organization, and performs trailer movements within the yard; this role is a candidate for substitution or assistance by autonomous robot tractors.

Each actor ensures that trailers are handled efficiently and safely, enabling on-time pickup and delivery, although their tasks differ in terms of cognitive and physical demands. Key activities include checking trailers for ID, destination, and condition; assigning docks based on schedule and availability; moving trailers, whether manually or with autonomous assistance; positioning trailers at docks, which often requires manual skill; and verifying cargo before and after transport. While automating trailer movement addresses physical demands, it introduces significant cognitive risks for the human supervisor. Long periods of monitoring routine, reliable autonomous operation can lead to vigilance decrement, impairing the operator's ability to detect system faults. Furthermore, the complexity of AI decision-making creates a risk of loss of SA, as the operator may not understand the robot's plan or state. When supervising multiple autonomous vehicles simultaneously, this lack of transparency and sustained monitoring also results in a high cognitive workload. By categorizing these activities, we can analyze how the robot tractor may be implemented on the site. For example, as shown in Fig. 1, trailer movement can be handled by the tractor, which will require human supervision, raising issues related to human roles, interface design, transparency, and cognitive load.

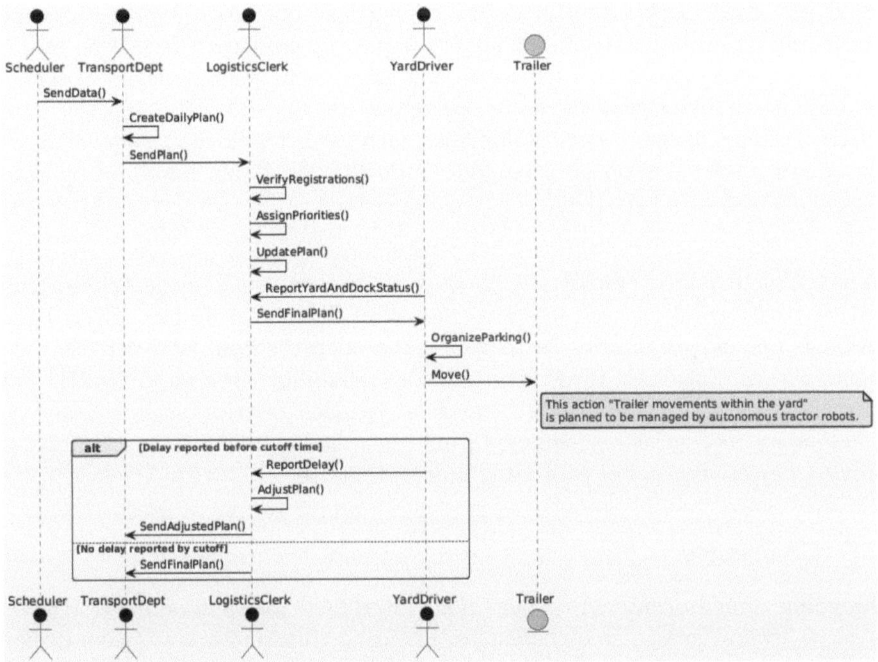

Fig. 1. Sequence diagram illustrating a possible scenario of trailer yard management.

4.2   Potential Applications

Building on the activity analysis, we now explore how each design guideline could inform potential interface features and workflows. These applications remain hypothetical, intended to illustrate how the framework might guide the design of human-centered supervision systems rather than represent deployed solutions.

Transparency and Situational Awareness. To set up transparency, operators should be able to develop and update their SA of the robots, i.e., perceive the robots' movements or status, to understand and anticipate their behaviors. For example, regarding the maneuver selection process, the interface must present high-fidelity rationales derived from the agent's internal policy structure. This structural approach supports Causal XAI by generating temporal counterfactual explanations that clarify goal selection and plan execution (e.g., "The tractor stopped because the safety constraint node was activated; if the obstacle had been 1 m further, the move node would have been selected"). This method provides decision traceability superior to model-agnostic techniques.

Cognitive Workload Management. To reduce operator overload, interfaces could prioritize alerts using event-driven notifications (e.g., highlighting only safety-critical events and minimizing lower-priority updates). It will be important to provide operators with tools that help them manage their workload. This approach aligns with the design principles developed for Human-AI Hybrid (HAH) systems in safety-critical domains, such as air traffic management, where systematic reviews emphasize dynamic authority allocation based on operator load and task complexity [26].

Trust Calibration. Validation of trust calibration must move beyond subjective trust scores to the objective metric of Trust Resolution. Trust Resolution is defined as the degree to which the operator's subjective trust judgments accurately reflect the system's actual reliability variability [10,25]. This requires empirical testing using behavioral reliance metrics, such as intervention latency and decision accuracy during controlled error injection scenarios, to provide objective proof of calibrated human reliance.

4.3   Challenges

Designing human-centered supervision interfaces for autonomous tractors presents several interrelated challenges. Ensuring transparency and goal display is difficult due to the complexity of AI decision-making and the risk of overwhelming supervisors with excessive or rapidly changing information [21,24]. Cognitive workload management requires prioritizing critical tasks and adapting information display in real-time, while effectively monitoring user stress and attention. Trust calibration is challenging because users may over- or under-rely on the AI, and explanations such as LIME, SHAP, or counterfactuals can be difficult for non-experts to interpret correctly. Cross-cutting issues include integrating new UIs with existing yard management systems, measuring performance across multiple dimensions (trust, workload, usability, and decision accuracy), and providing sufficient training to ensure supervisors understand and appropriately act on AI outputs.

5   Discussion

The proposed work builds on insights from HCI, human factors, and XAI research to argue that current approaches to supervising autonomous logistics tractors are insufficiently human-centered. While safety has been the dominant focus in recent studies, ergonomics, usability, and trust have received comparatively less attention. By framing supervision through principles such as workload management, transparency, and trust calibration, this paper advocates for a more balanced approach to system design.

While the three design considerations (transparency and SA, cognitive workload management, and trust calibration) draw on established ergonomics, HCI, and HRI principles, their implementation requires their contextualization and adaptation to autonomous tractor supervision. Through activity analysis and designactivity mapping, these principles must be operationalized for domain-specific supervision needs, bridging empirical workflow understanding with theoretical design heuristics. The result is a set of actionable, novel guidance comprising specific, prescriptive design mandates necessary to safely and effectively integrate AI supervision into a real-world logistics environment, moving beyond generalized theory. Table 1 summarizes how the proposed framework extends the classical principles and communicates both empirical grounding and novelty.

Table 1. Examples of application of the three principles to autonomous tractors supervision.

Classic HCI/HRI Principle	Domain-Specific Adaptation (The proposed framework)	Example of application
Transparency and Situational Awareness	Causal XAI-based transparency for decision traceability	Tractor stops unexpectedly
Cognitive Workload Management	Adaptive notification prioritization	Supervising multiple tractors
Trust Calibration	Continuous trust feedback loop via uncertainty displays	Anomaly handling

Traditional transparency paradigms in XAI, designed for static classification tasks, are insufficient for autonomous planning agents. The opacity issue lies not only in the black-box nature of the models, but also in the potential misalignment between the agent's internal policy and goals and those of the human supervisor. Integrating causal reasoning and counterfactual explanations into supervision interfaces addresses this challenge, enabling operators to understand not only what actions occurred but also why specific plans were selected and how deviations relate to operational constraints or anomalies.

The activity analysis of a mid-sized logistics hub highlighted the role of the human operator in the supervision of robot tractors in logistics platform operations. For example, this role is crucial for anomaly handling and judgment under uncertainty.

A key implication of our work is that design should move beyond focusing solely on *what robots can do* to consider *how humans can supervise and collaborate effectively.* In this perspective, HITL supervision is therefore positioned not as a fallback for failure but as a proactive design principle that supports resilient, ergonomic, and trustworthy interaction. A possible future direction for this framework involves integrating Large Language Models (LLMs) into the supervisory system's architecture. LLMs are uniquely capable of functioning as high-level agent coordinators in the logistics workflow, managing complex operations like dynamic scheduling, task decomposition, and fleet-wide constraint handling. Crucially, LLMs can be leveraged downstream to process the complex, technical output of the Structural Causal XAI model (e.g., the activated BT nodes) and translate it into adaptive, natural language, human-readable explanations for supervisors [15]. This synthesis may allow the system to convey the technical *why* in a concise, human-centric format, filtering complexity to directly support the Cognitive Workload Management principle and enhancing overall operator understanding. It should be noted, however, that LLMs are likely to produce "hallucinations" which should be mitigated.

In addition, integrating causal inference into XAI-based supervision offers a promising direction regarding transparency. Causal explanations can provide counterfactual reasoning, clarifying not only *why* an autonomous decision occurred but also *how* outcomes would have differed under alternative conditions. This approach may enhance the interpretability of system actions and can significantly strengthen operator trust in complex or ambiguous situations involving the robot tractors.

Finally, our work underscores the importance of interdisciplinary approaches. Combining ergonomics, HITL, HCI, HRI, and XAI techniques can guide the design of autonomous tractor monitoring systems involving human operators.

6   Conclusion

Adopting a human-centered design philosophy is not merely beneficial but essential for the successful integration of autonomous robot tractors into the complex, dynamic environments of modern logistics platforms. By synthesizing theoretical insights from diverse fields, including cognitive ergonomics, HITL methodologies, HCI, HRI, and XAI, we have identified three interrelated design considerations that are critical for effective supervision: the enhancement of *transparency and SA*, the active regulation of *cognitive workload*, and the precise *calibration of operator trust*.

Our future research agenda will focus on the rigorous operationalization of this framework. This process will begin with a detailed specification of supervision tasks to map the distinct informational needs of human operators. We will subsequently conduct iterative participatory design sessions involving experienced logistics operators to empirically validate these needs and co-design the interface. These sessions will inform the development of a high-fidelity proof of concept featuring a guarded LLM pipeline. This mechanism will be strictly constrained to log-verified data to mitigate the risk of "hallucinations", ensuring that the system supports preventive, rather than merely reactive, safety interventions.

Finally, we will evaluate the system through a comprehensive empirical user evaluation. We will explore the relevance of the Situation Awareness Global Assessment Technique (SAGAT) to assess the accuracy of the operator's cognitive model of the situation, the NASA-TLX index to analyse cognitive workload, and specific behavioral metrics, such as intervention latency and accuracy, to assess trust calibration. These combined efforts will serve to refine our conceptual framework and ensure that human-centred supervision remains practical, effective, and robust enough to adapt to the rapidly evolving landscape of industrial automation.

References

1. Adebayo, A., Ajayi, O., Chukwurah, N., Pub, A.: Explainable ai in robotics: a critical review and implementation strategies for transparent decision-making. J. Multidisciplinary Res. **05**, 26–32 (2024)
2. Bhattathiri, S., et al.: Unlocking human-robot synergy: the power of intent communication in warehouse robotics. Appl. Ergon. **117**, 104248 (2024). https://doi.org/10.1016/j.apergo.2024.104248
3. Chen, Y., Yang, C., Song, B., Gonzalez, N., Gu, Y., Hu, B.: Effects of autonomous mobile robots on human mental workload and system productivity in smart warehouses: a preliminary study. In: Proceedings of the Human Factors and Ergonomics Society Annual Meeting, vol. 64, no. 1, pp. 1691–1695 (2020). https://doi.org/10.1177/1071181320641410. https://journals.sagepub.com/doi/abs/10.1177/1071181320641410
4. Colceriu, C., Theis, S., Brell-Cokcan, S., Nitsch, V.: User-centered design in mobile human-robot cooperation: consideration of usability and situation awareness in GUI design for mobile robots at assembly workplaces. i-com **22**(3), 193–213 (2023). https://doi.org/10.1515/icom-2023-0016
5. Daniellou, F., Rabardel, P.: Activity-oriented approaches to ergonomics: some traditions and communities. Theor. Issues Ergon. Sci. **6**(5), 353–357 (2005). https://doi.org/10.1080/14639220500078351
6. Endsley, M.: Toward a theory of situation awareness in dynamic systems. Hum. Factors: J. Hum. Factors Ergon. Soc. **37**, 32–64 (1995). https://doi.org/10.1518/001872095779049543
7. Fröhlich, P., Mirnig, A., Zafari, S., Baldauf, M.: The human in the loop in automated production processes: terminology, aspects and current challenges in HCI research. In: CEUR workshop at CHI23; CHI 2023 - ACM CHI Conference on Human Factors in Computing Systems, 23–27 April 2023, vol. 3394 (2023). https://chi2023.acm.org/
8. Haney, J., Liang, C.J.: A literature review on safety perception and trust during human-robot interaction with autonomous mobile robots that apply to industrial environments. IISE Trans. Occupational Ergon. Hum. Factors **12**, 1–22 (2024). https://doi.org/10.1080/24725838.2023.2283537
9. Kaindl, H., Svetinovic, D.: Avoiding undertrust and overtrust. In: Joint Proceedings of REFSQ-2019 Workshops with the 25th International Conference on Requirements Engineering: Foundation for Software Quality, Essen, Germany. CEUR Workshop Proceedings, vol. 2376. CEUR-WS (2019), publisher Copyright: Copyright © 2019 by the paper's authors.; 2019 Joint of International Conference on Requirements Engineering: Foundation for Software Quality Workshops, Doctoral Symposium, Live Studies Track, and Poster Track, REFSQ-JP 2019 ; Conference date: 18-03-2019
10. Lee, J.D., See, K.A.: Trust in automation: designing for appropriate reliance. Hum. Factors J. Hum. Factors Ergon. Soc. **46**(1), 50–80 (2004)
11. Love, T., Andriella, A., Alenyà, G.: Temporal counterfactual explanations of behaviour tree decisions (2025). https://doi.org/10.48550/arXiv.2509.07674

12. Mualla, Y.: Explaining the behavior of remote robots to humans: an agent-based approach. Theses, Université Bourgogne Franche-Comté (2020). https://tel.archives-ouvertes.fr/tel-03162833
13. Mualla, Y., et al.: The quest of parsimonious XAI: a human-agent architecture for explanation formulation. Artif. Intell. **302**, 103573 (2022). https://doi.org/10.1016/j.artint.2021.103573. https://www.sciencedirect.com/science/article/pii/S0004370221001247
14. Norman, D.: Design of everyday things (1988)
15. Picard, A., Mualla, Y., Gechter, F.: Explaining in natural language: a discussion on leveraging the reasoning capabilities of LLMs for XAI. In: Joint Proceedings of the xAI 2025 Late-breaking Work, Demos and Doctoral Consortium co-located with the 3rd World Conference on eXplainable Artificial Intelligence (xAI 2025), Istanbul, Turkey, 9–11 July 2025. CEUR Workshop Proceedings, vol. 4017, pp. 161–168. CEUR-WS.org (2025). https://ceur-ws.org/Vol-4017/paper_21.pdf
16. Picard, A., Mualla, Y., Gechter, F., Galland, S.: Human-computer interaction and explainability: intersection and terminology. In: Longo, L. (ed.) Explainable Artificial Intelligence - First World Conference, xAI 2023, Lisbon, Portugal, 26–28 July 2023, Proceedings, Part II. Communications in Computer and Information Science, vol. 1902, pp. 214–236. Springer, Cham (2023). https://doi.org/10.1007/978-3-031-44067-0_12
17. Sakai, T., Nagai, T.: Explainable autonomous robots: a survey and perspective. Adv. Robot. **36**(5–6), 219–238 (2022). https://doi.org/10.1080/01691864.2022.2029720
18. Sanneman, L., Shah, J.: The situation awareness framework for explainable AI (safe-AI) and human factors considerations for XAI systems. Int. J. Hum.-Comput. Interact. **38**, 1–17 (2022). https://doi.org/10.1080/10447318.2022.2081282
19. Scapin, D.L., Bastien, J.M.C.: Ergonomic criteria for evaluating the ergonomic quality of interactive systems. Behav. Inf. Technol. **16**(4–5), 220–231 (1997). https://doi.org/10.1080/014492997119806
20. Sheridan, T.B.: Human–robot interaction: status and challenges. Hum. Factors **58**(4), 525–532 (2016). https://doi.org/10.1177/0018720816644364, pMID: 27098262
21. Shneiderman, B.: Human-centered artificial intelligence: Reliable, safe & trustworthy. Int. J. Hum.-Comput. Interact. **36**(6), 495–504 (2020). https://doi.org/10.1080/10447318.2020.1741118
22. Simões, A., Pinto, A., Santos, J., Pinheiro, S., Romero, D.: Designing human-robot collaboration (HRC) workspaces in industrial settings: a systematic literature review. J. Manuf. Syst. **62**, 28–43 (2022). https://doi.org/10.1016/j.jmsy.2021.11.007
23. Sreedharan, S., Chakraborti, T., Kambhampati, S.: Foundations of explanations as model reconciliation. Artif. Intell. **301**, 103558 (2021). https://doi.org/10.1016/j.artint.2021.103558. https://www.sciencedirect.com/science/article/pii/S0004370221001090
24. Valentine, D.C., Smit, I., Kim, E.: Designing for calibrated trust: exploring the challenges in calibrating trust between users and autonomous vehicles. Proc. Des. Soc. **1**, 1143–1152 (2021). https://doi.org/10.1017/pds.2021.114
25. Wiegmann, D., McCarley, J.S., Shappell, S.: Defining and measuring trust and reliance in human-autonomy teaming. Front. Psychol. **11**, 577 (2020)
26. Xia, Z., et al.: A systematic review on human-ai hybrid systems and human factors in air traffic management. J. Eng. Des. **36**(6), 357–382 (2025). https://doi.org/10.1080/09544828.2025.2509056

ROXIE: Defining a Robotic eXplanation and Interpretability Engine

Francisco J. Rodríguez Lera[1]([envelope]) [ORCID], Miguel Ángel González-Santamarta[1] [ORCID],
Alejandro González-Cantón[1] [ORCID], Laura Fernández Becerra[1] [ORCID],
David Sobrín Hidalgo[1] [ORCID], Ángel Manuel Guerrero-Higueras[1] [ORCID],
and Irene González Fernández[2] [ORCID]

[1] Grupo de Robótica, Instituto I4, Universidad de León, León, Spain
`fjrodl@unileon.es`
[2] Intelligent Robotics Lab, Universidad Rey Juan Carlos, Madrid, Spain

Abstract. As autonomous robots become more prevalent in public environments, ensuring the transparency and interpretability of their decision-making processes is crucial to building trust and promoting effective human-robot collaboration. The European Union's Artificial Intelligence Act (AI Act) reinforces these priorities by establishing a regulatory framework that emphasizes accountability, explainability, and ethical governance in AI systems. In this context, this paper presents the Robotic eXplanation and Interpretability Engine (ROXIE) a framework specifically designed to address these challenges by clarifying and making understandable the complex behaviors exhibited by autonomous robots.

ROXIE defines the essential requirements for explainability and interpretability while leveraging the tools, components, and libraries available within the ROS 2 ecosystem to implement these capabilities in a practical and scalable manner. By providing clear, accessible, and context-aware explanations of robotic decision-making, ROXIE bridges the gap between technical innovation and regulatory compliance. Ultimately, it contributes to the responsible deployment of autonomous systems, fostering transparency, trust, and societal acceptance in the emerging era of explainable robotics.

Keywords: ROS 2 · Regulation 2024/1689 · Explainability · Accountability

1 Introduction

The integration of autonomous robots into public spaces, such as airports and hospitals, poses significant challenges that require mechanisms to ensure transparency, accountability, and trust in their decision-making processes. The European Union's Artificial Intelligence Act (AI Act), Regulation (EU) 2024/1689, introduces stringent requirements for high-risk AI systems, including autonomous robots operating in public spaces. These requirements explicitly mandate transparency, explainability, and human oversight of AI systems, particularly when they interact directly with citizens.

This paper addresses these regulatory challenges by proposing ROXIE, a framework for explainability and interpretability tailored to autonomous robots and explicitly aligned with the AI Act's requirements. Our framework specifically addresses:

- Article 13 (Transparency): through real-time explainable behaviors and clear documentation
- Article 14 (Human Oversight): by providing multi-level explanations adapted to different stakeholders
- Article 15 (Accuracy and Robustness): via traceable decision-making processes and accountability measures
- Article 17 (Data Quality): through our data management and logging approaches

By focusing on these regulatory requirements while leveraging existing tools and techniques within the ROS 2 ecosystem, ROXIE provides a practical pathway for developing compliant autonomous robots. This approach bridges the gap between theoretical insights and practical applications, enabling the deployment of robots that are not only efficient but also understandable, trustworthy, and legally compliant.

By grounding the framework in the context of evolving legal and technical standards, this work offers a pathway for assessing and improving the transparency of autonomous systems, ensuring their alignment with societal values and regulatory requirements.

1.1   Contribution

This paper introduces a requirements-driven framework for explainability, interpretability, and accountability in autonomous robotic systems, addressing both theoretical foundations and practical deployment concerns. The proposed framework seeks to tackle key challenges faced by the robotics community, including:

- Defining a structured set of requirements for explainability, interpretability, and accountability in autonomous robots operating across diverse and regulated scenarios.
- Organizing existing techniques and tools within the ROS 2 ecosystem according to these requirements, enabling their systematic integration into robotic architectures.

Beyond a purely technical perspective, this work explicitly aligns the proposed framework with emerging regulatory and standardization efforts, such as the EU Artificial Intelligence Act and ISO/IEC 42001:2023. By doing so, it contributes a coherent foundation for the development, assessment, and standardization of trustworthy robotic systems that are transparent, accountable, and suitable for real-world deployment.

The remainder of the paper is organized as follows: Sect. 2 presents a comprehensive review of relevant literature on explainable robotics and interpretable AI systems. Section 3 provides an overview of ROXIE and its key components. Section 4 details our initial implementation and proof of concept using ROS 2 tools. Finally, Sect. 5 presents conclusions and directions for future work.

2   Related Work

A recurring source of ambiguity in the robotics and AI literature is the overlap between *explainability* and *interpretability*. Following Rudin [20], interpretable systems make their decision-making processes understandable by design, whereas explainable systems provide post-hoc accounts of otherwise opaque models. In human–robot interaction, explanations must also account for the communication process itself and the needs of the receiver, as structured by Anjomshoae et al.'s generation–communication–reception loop [1]. These perspectives motivate our separation of ROXIE's interpretability (RIFT) and explainability (REFT) toolkits, as well as the role-adaptive presentation requirement (R0.2).

Model-agnostic methods such as SHAP [14] and LIME [19], together with deep-learning attribution libraries like Captum [11] and Layerwise Relevance Propagation (LRP), provide feature- and instance-level rationales for image, text, and tabular inputs. Recent advances in Large Language Models (LLMs) and multimodal architectures such as LLaVA [13] and GPT-4V have enabled more natural and context-aware explanations of robot behavior. These models can process multiple input modalities (visual, textual, sensory) and generate human-like explanations that adapt to the user's level of expertise. In embodied settings, these techniques have been employed to highlight perceptual evidence (e.g., on top of detectors such as YOLOv8 [10]) and to surface salient internal signals that drive downstream decisions. However, their raw outputs are rarely intelligible to non-experts, reinforcing the need for translation layers that adapt both content and granularity to different stakeholders [1].

Robotic platforms expose a rich set of dynamic and static sources of evidence. Dynamic evidence includes runtime visualizations (e.g., behavior-tree and FSM viewers such as Groot and YASMIN, or data dashboards like Foxglove [2,4,7]) and high-volume logs. Recent work combines logs with Large Language Models (LLMs) to summarize and contextualize behavior, often through Retrieval-Augmented Generation to focus on relevant events [12,21,22]. Static evidence spans configurations and algorithms (e.g., ROS 2 and Navigation2 parameters, planners, and controllers [15,16]), datasets, and trained models; tracking their provenance and runtime changes is essential for providing faithful and verifiable accounts of robot behavior.

Beyond online explanations, accountability requires durable and tamper-evident records to support incident analysis and assurance. Ethical Black Box proposals advocate standardized recording of sensor data, actuator commands, and internal system states [28]. Complementary approaches provide *Accountability as a Service*, enabling secure and privacy-preserving event capture and analysis [3, 26]. Such mechanisms are becoming increasingly critical as regulatory frameworks governing autonomous systems continue to evolve.

The EU AI Act (Regulation (EU) 2024/1689) represents a major milestone in AI governance, with direct implications for the design and deployment of autonomous robotic systems. In particular, Article 13 mandates transparency obligations for high-risk AI systems, while Article 14 explicitly requires the provision of effective human oversight mechanisms. Together, these provisions establish explainability and interpretability as core regulatory requirements rather than optional system features.

Complementing this regulatory framework, the IEEE P7001 standard for transparency in autonomous systems [27] provides practical guidance on how transparency should be operationalized, emphasizing the need for explanations adapted to different stakeholders and contexts of use. In parallel, the ISO/IEC 42001:2023 standard [9] introduces the first international requirements for an Artificial Intelligence Management System (AIMS), promoting organizational-level governance practices for responsible, transparent, and accountable AI throughout its lifecycle.

Taken together, these regulatory and standardization efforts are accelerating the integration of explainability, interpretability, and accountability mechanisms directly into robotic architectures, reinforcing the need for systematic frameworks that address both technical and organizational dimensions of trustworthy autonomous systems.

Despite significant progress, current deployments remain fragmented: (i) attribution tools are seldom integrated end-to-end with robotic software stacks; (ii) evidence collection lacks consistent schemas across perception, planning, and control components; (iii) explanations are rarely adapted to user roles in real time; and (iv) accountability mechanisms are not consistently coupled to explanation pipelines. ROXIE addresses these gaps through a requirements-driven architecture: REFT to extract and curate explanations from heterogeneous sources, RIFT to measure and enhance the interpretability of models and components, and RAFT to ensure secure and standardized recording for audit and post-incident analysis.

3   ROXIE

The acronym ROXIE, which stands for *Robotic eXplanation and Interpretability Engine*, encapsulates a holistic strategy aimed at addressing the challenges posed by the inherent opacity of complex robotic decision-making processes. In essence, ROXIE embodies a comprehensive and systematic approach to unraveling these intricacies and enhancing the transparency of decision-making within autonomous robotic systems. Accordingly, ROXIE defines three main toolkits:

- REFT: Robotic Explanation Framework Toolkit
- RIFT: Robotic Interpretability Framework Toolkit
- RAFT: Robotic Accountability Framework Toolkit

The term *Framework Toolkit* refers here to a collection of tools, resources, and components bundled together to facilitate the development, implementation, and maintenance of software applications. Typical elements of such a toolkit include code libraries, documentation, templates and normalized proposals, integrated development environments (IDEs), command-line tools, testing utilities, and debugging mechanisms. These components are expected to be supported by an active community.

At the same time, the robotics community often uses the terms *explainability* and *interpretability* interchangeably. Drawing from machine learning research, Rudin [20] establishes a clear boundary between interpretable and explainable machine learning (ML). Interpretable ML prioritizes the design of models that are inherently understandable, whereas explainable ML focuses on providing retrospective explanations for pre-existing black-box models. In the context of explainable robotics, this work follows Pennington's model of explanation-based decision-making [17], in which an explanation is understood as a mental representation of a situation relevant to a decision-making process, emphasizing events, conditions, and relationships.

Figure 1 provides an overview of the full set of requirements necessary to achieve an explainable and interpretable engine. The engine is intentionally defined in terms of requirements rather than concrete components, since many of these requirements may be realized through multiple software modules.

Two basic requirements are considered transversal to all others, as they underpin trust, accountability, and regulatory compliance across the entire ROXIE architecture:

R0.1 **Cybersecurity:** All ROXIE components, both hardware and software, must adhere to fundamental cybersecurity principles, ensuring the confidentiality, integrity, and availability of all data collected, processed, or generated by the robot. This requirement is essential not only for protecting the system against tampering or unauthorized access, but also for preserving the reliability of the evidence used for explainability and accountability. Secure logging, anti-tampering mechanisms, controlled access, backup strategies, and physical protection are therefore integral elements of ROXIE. In this sense, cybersecurity acts as an enabling condition for trustworthy transparency and is closely aligned with the safety and robustness obligations stated in Article 15 of the EU AI Act, as well as with the governance-oriented risk management principles of ISO/IEC 42001:2023.

R0.2 **Natural Language Interaction:** ROXIE must present information to humans in an intelligible and context-aware manner, prioritizing natural language as the primary communication medium. This requirement addresses the fact that raw technical artifacts, such as encrypted logs, internal state variables, or low-level system messages, are insufficient for meaningful human understanding, particularly for non-expert users. Natural language explanations constitute a key mechanism for fulfilling the transparency and human

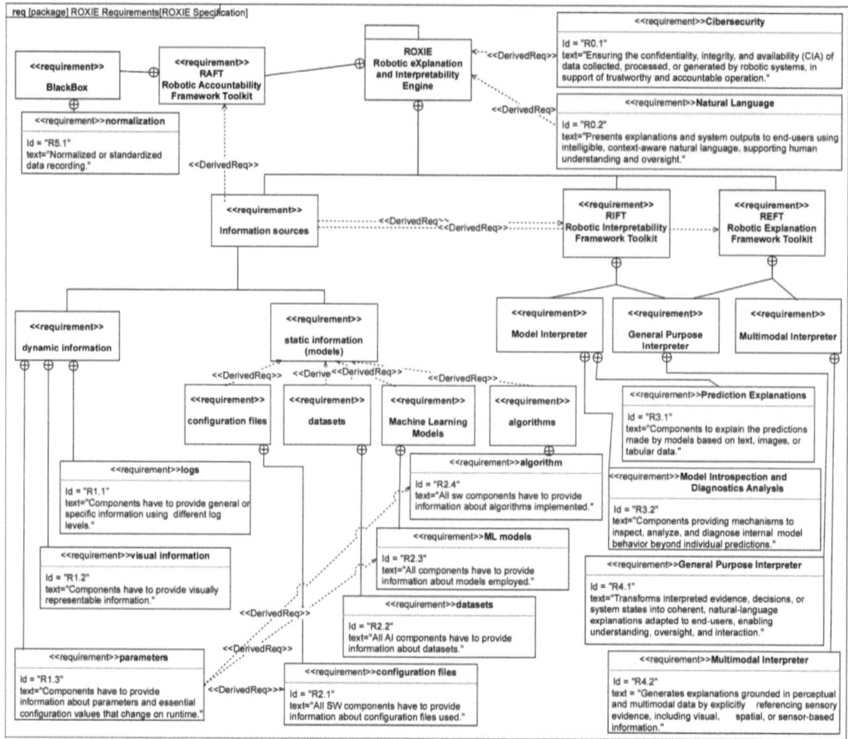

Fig. 1. Robotic eXplanation and Interpretability Engine (ROXIE) requirement definition. The diagram illustrates the hierarchical organization of requirements and their relationships across information sources, interpretability (RIFT), explainability (REFT), and accountability (RAFT). Derived requirements and dependency relationships are explicitly represented.

oversight obligations of Articles 13 and 14 of the EU AI Act, as well as the human-centered operation principles promoted by ISO/IEC 42001:2023. By translating technical evidence into accessible explanations, ROXIE enables informed interaction, appropriate oversight, and calibrated trust.

Roboticists and developers must regard these two requirements as foundational. A system whose data or behavior can be altered without traceability, or whose internal processes cannot be communicated in an understandable way, cannot be considered trustworthy. Compromised integrity undermines accountability, while unclear or overly technical communication may mislead users or hinder effective human–robot interaction, ultimately weakening confidence in the system's behavior and decisions.

3.1   Information Sources

Information sources constitute a core requirement for any autonomous robot. In an explainable and interpretable engine, their importance lies in ensuring transparency, accountability, and a clear understanding of the system's decision-making process.

Knowing the sources of information enables users, stakeholders, and regulators to understand how decisions are produced by the system. Identifiable information sources contribute directly to accountability: when a decision is questioned or challenged, traceability allows biases, errors, or problematic data to be identified.

Understanding the information associated with data sources also supports continuous monitoring and updating, enabling error correction, data quality improvements, and overall performance enhancement. For end-users or non-experts interacting with the engine, insight into information sources facilitates a higher-level understanding of system behavior. Users are more likely to engage with and trust a system when they can grasp the basis of its decisions, even without detailed technical knowledge.

Finally, ethical considerations are increasingly relevant as AI systems impact multiple domains of society. Visibility into information sources supports fairness and helps prevent discriminatory outcomes. Moreover, regulatory frameworks often mandate transparency and explainability in AI systems, and clear documentation of information sources directly contributes to compliance.

3.1.1   Dynamic Information

Dynamic information sources include all data that change at runtime. These sources can be broadly categorized into visual information and logs generated by software components.

R1.1 **Visual Information:** Robotic systems typically provide multiple visualization tools that offer insight into ongoing processes. These viewers present robot behavior using high-level representations that allow developers and operators to understand system execution. Examples include finite state machine visualizers such as YASMIN [7] and behavior tree viewers such as Groot [2]. Additional tools include ROS computational graph visualizations and advanced platforms such as Foxglove [4], an open-source visualization and debugging tool for robotic data.

R1.2 **Logs:** Logs constitute a common information source for explaining robot behavior. In prior work, logs have been combined with Large Language Models (LLMs) to generate explanations for autonomous robots. However, as the number of software components increases, the volume of generated logs also grows significantly. To address this challenge, recent work [22] leverages Retrieval-Augmented Generation (RAG) [12], a prompt engineering technique [21] used to retrieve only the most relevant log entries.

R1.3 **Parameters:** Parameters are configurable settings of software components that can be adjusted during execution. For example, navigation parameters such as maximum speed may be modified to adapt to different environments. Similarly, machine learning models may update weights at runtime, such as dynamically adjusting object detection models to recognize different object classes. Tracking these changes is essential for explaining observed robot behavior.

3.1.2   Static Information

Static information sources include all elements that do not change during execution. These encompass configuration files, datasets, machine learning models, and algorithms.

R2.1 **Configuration Files:** Configuration files define aspects of software behavior in autonomous robots. Although static at runtime, they exert substantial influence on system behavior. A representative example is found in the ROS 2 Navigation2 framework [16], where configuration files define parameters such as maximum velocity, global planning strategies, and controller selection.

R2.2 **Datasets:** Datasets provide static information used to train machine learning models embedded in autonomous robots. While immutable during execution, they critically shape robot behavior and decision-making, making them essential for explaining system actions.

R2.3 **Machine Learning Models:** Trained models, including deep learning architectures, act as static repositories of knowledge. Although their parameters remain fixed during execution, they strongly influence perception and decision-making. For instance, integrating YOLOv8 [6,10] enables robots to extract semantic information from visual input.

R2.4 **Algorithms:** Algorithms represent static software components governing robot functionality. These include navigation plugins in Nav2, finite state machines such as YASMIN [7], and other core robotic modules.

Although static, these elements are often associated with parameters that evolve over time (R1.2). Tracking such changes is therefore necessary to guarantee transparency in robot behavior.

3.2   RIFT

The Robotic Interpretability Framework Toolkit (RIFT) comprises tools, methodologies, and components designed to support the development, implementation, and assessment of decision-making processes in autonomous robots. Interpretability in robotics refers to the extent to which humans—users, operators, or other stakeholders—can understand and reason about the decisions and actions taken by a robotic system.

The level of interpretability depends on the transparency of internal models, the availability of static and dynamic information, and the overall system complexity. These factors must be measured and evaluated to foster transparency and trust between robots and humans.

While interpretability and explainability are often conflated, they serve distinct roles. Interpretability refers to the inherent transparency of a system's decision-making mechanisms, whereas explainability focuses on generating post-hoc explanations that translate complex processes into human-understandable terms.

A key challenge of interpretability is its subjective nature: what is interpretable for one user may be incomprehensible to another, depending on technical background and domain expertise. Information may be conveyed through logs, graphs, or natural language, but its effectiveness depends on the user's familiarity with these representations. Recent advances in Large Language Models offer promising mechanisms for adapting explanations to diverse user profiles.

Interpretability is essential for building trust in robotic systems, as it provides direct insight into their behavior. However, to be effective, information must be adapted to the knowledge level of its audience, as required by R0.2, thereby establishing a strong link between RIFT and REFT.

Two primary requirements are associated with RIFT and are closely connected to REFT:

R3.1 **Prediction Explanation:** Components should be capable of explaining predictions derived from image, text, or tabular data, providing insight into the robot's cognitive processes by clarifying why and how specific outputs are generated.

R3.2 **Model Introspection and Diagnostic Analysis:** Components should provide mechanisms to inspect, analyze, and diagnose the internal behavior of models beyond individual predictions. This includes ad hoc analysis, sensitivity studies, gradient-based inspection, and intermediate representation analysis, enabling developers and auditors to understand model behavior, limitations, and failure modes.

Applying these techniques to system logs, for example, can highlight the most relevant messages during an action. Tools widely used in the AI community, such as SHAP [14] and LIME [19], can also be applied in robotics to identify salient elements influencing predictions. These models should provide metrics or explanatory representations that reflect the underlying decision process.

To enhance comprehensibility, the use of a General Purpose Interpreter (defined in REFT) is required. Explanations should follow the three phases identified by Anjomshoae et al. [1]: explanation generation, explanation communication, and explanation reception.

3.3 REFT

This toolkit provides tools, resources, and methodologies to facilitate the creation and integration of explanations in robotic decision-making processes. Within ROXIE, it is essential to clarify the conceptual boundary between RIFT and REFT. RIFT focuses on interpretability by exposing, inspecting, and analyzing internal models, data, and decision processes, thereby providing evidence about how and why system behavior emerges. REFT, by contrast, addresses explainability by transforming this evidence into intelligible and context-aware explanations tailored to human stakeholders. In this sense, RIFT operates on internal representations and evidence, whereas REFT operates on their communication and presentation.

Typically, decision-making processes in autonomous robots are executed in a manner that is non-transparent to the user. The evidence produced by RIFT must therefore be processed and curated by REFT using explainability algorithms or machine learning techniques. These techniques may rely on quantitative metrics, visualizations of internal system states, or detected relevant events generated by RIFT, and transform them into human-understandable explanations of cognitive functions such as perception, deliberative reasoning, or action control. The goal of REFT is to enable explainability by ensuring that such evidence is rendered intelligible to end-users through appropriate interpretative mechanisms. At this stage, two main components are defined: the Multimodal Interpreter and the General Purpose Interpreter.

R4.1 **General Purpose Interpreter:** A component responsible for translating interpreted evidence, decisions, and internal system states into coherent, natural-language explanations adapted to end-user requirements. Its role is to generate structured, context-aware narratives that support understanding, oversight, and interaction.

R4.2 **Multimodal Interpreter:** A specialized component focused on grounding explanations in perceptual and multimodal data, such as images, sensor streams, or combined visualtextual representations. It enables the generation of explanations that explicitly reference perceptual evidence (e.g., visual regions, objects, or spatial relations) and supports multimodal explanation outputs.

While the General Purpose Interpreter focuses on linguistic and narrative explanations, the Multimodal Interpreter provides grounding by explicitly linking explanations to perceptual and sensory evidence.

The General Purpose Interpreter is required in both REFT and RIFT and is directly linked to R0.2. Explanations are conceived as structured collections of statements comprising facts, beliefs, rules, contextual information, causal clarifications, and potential consequences, in line with state-of-the-art approaches [1].

3.4 RAFT

The Robotic Accountability Framework Toolkit (RAFT) provides guidelines, tools, and resources to ensure ethical, responsible, and transparent design, development, and deployment of robotic systems. RAFT addresses accountability from multiple perspectives, including ethics, legal compliance, safety, transparency, and cybersecurity.

A key requirement is the inclusion of a component analogous to an aircraft Flight Data Recorder, capable of recording sensor data, actuator behavior, and relevant internal system states. This functionality is essential for accident and incident investigation, particularly as robots move beyond controlled laboratory environments.

R5.1 A standardized approach to data recording should enable consistent and efficient investigation of robotic accidents and incidents, while supporting interoperability and adaptability across platforms.

Both industry and research communities have proposed solutions in this direction. While implementations need not be unique, they should share standard mechanisms for recording and communication with external systems [28]. Standard specifications, such as those proposed by Winfield [28], facilitate the sharing and adaptation of black box implementations across robotic platforms, fostering interoperability and encouraging broader adoption.

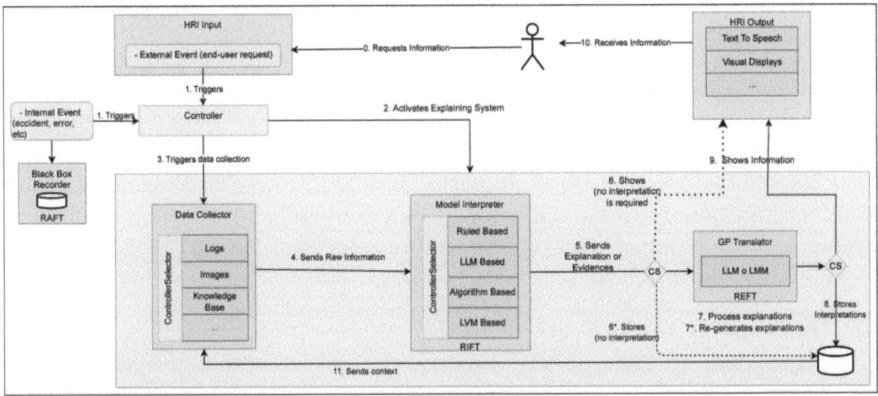

Fig. 2. Example of ROXIE concept integration in a real robot, presented through the XENIA system.

4 Proof of Concept

In the development of an explicable robotic system, the integration of versatile tools plays a pivotal role in ensuring the system's ability to provide effective explanations. This section explores the practical application of the concepts introduced earlier within a robotic system, focusing on state-of-the-art solutions employed in our research.

4.1 Description and Case Study

To illustrate how ROXIE operates in a real-world scenario, we consider a service robot operating in a hospital environment, tasked with delivering medical supplies between different departments. This example demonstrates how the framework manages both routine operations and unexpected situations while providing appropriate explanations to different stakeholders.

Consider a scenario in which the robot must transport urgent medical supplies from the pharmacy to the emergency department. During its journey, it encounters a temporarily blocked corridor and is required to recalculate its route. This situation involves multiple stakeholders (medical staff, patients, and visitors) and demands different levels of explanation depending on the user's role and technical expertise.

In this case, ROXIE provides:

- For medical staff: Detailed status updates regarding delivery timing and route changes, including explicit reasons for any delays.
- For patients and visitors: Simple and clear explanations about the robot's current task and movement decisions.
- For technical staff: Detailed logs and system state information to support troubleshooting and system optimization.

Before implementing the explanation flow in a real robot, it is essential to define the temporal scope of the explainability process. Two complementary perspectives can be distinguished in explainable robotic systems: online (real-time) and offline (non-real-time). Integrating ROXIE into a real-world robot may introduce additional computational load that could affect performance in public environments, making careful design decisions necessary.

The online approach can be addressed from two complementary angles:

(i) **Inherent ROXIE System:** Real-time presentation of information. This corresponds to the traditional approach used to monitor robot execution, typically relying on visualization tools such as RViz, Groot, or the YASMIN viewer.

(ii) **Post-hoc ROXIE System:** Real-time analysis decoupled from the audited system, combined with privacy-preserving mechanisms. These features are particularly desirable in accountability-oriented approaches. For instance, the authors in [3] propose an Accountability as a Service (AaaS) framework based on recording and filtering system calls and their arguments executed by the monitored system. This solution also incorporates end-to-end encryption, thereby ensuring secure logging of executed events while facilitating subsequent analysis.

By contrast, the offline approach relies on previously stored data, typically obtained from rosbags or accountability mechanisms such as robotic black boxes.

4.2 Flow

In autonomous robotics, effective human–robot interaction depends critically on the robot's ability to provide transparent and comprehensible explanations for its actions. Achieving this objective requires the development and integration of a ROXIE-based approach, exemplified here through XENIA, a concrete system-level instantiation of the ROXIE requirements used to illustrate the explanation flow.

By detailing each stage of the process, we aim to clarify how XENIA's components operate in concert to enhance interpretability, foster user trust, and support meaningful human–robot interaction. Figure 2 presents our initial approach to deploying ROXIE concepts in robotic platforms.

(i) **User requests information:** The process begins with a user query, which initiates a sequence of events leading to the generation of explanations. This interaction acts as the primary trigger for the system, prompting engagement with multiple components to address the request. In addition to explicit user queries, internal system events may also activate the explainability mechanisms.

(ii) **System triggers XENIA:** Upon receiving the triggering event, the system activates XENIA, the ROXIE-based explanation and interpretability layer responsible for managing the explanation flow. This activation initiates the subsequent stages of explanation generation and interpretation. Depending on the lifecycle state of the system, XENIA may be activated or deactivated dynamically.

(iii) **Activation of the explaining system:** Once XENIA is active, the explaining system begins orchestrating the information flow and computational processes required to generate coherent explanations. This step marks the formal start of the explanation generation process, providing insights into the robot's decision-making.

(iv) **Triggering data collection:** To ensure comprehensive coverage, the system activates dormant data collection mechanisms and gathers non-default information sources. By incorporating additional data streams, the system enriches its understanding of the contextual factors surrounding the query.

(v) **System sends data to RIFT:** As data collection progresses, the gathered information is transmitted to the Robotic Interpretability Framework Toolkit (RIFT). Within RIFT, the Model Interpreter processes incoming data streams and extracts insights that inform subsequent stages of the pipeline.

(vi) **Controller Selector manages data flow:** After processing within RIFT, the Controller Selector manages the internal distribution of information. It distinguishes between data that must be sent directly to the Human–Machine Interface (HMI), data to be stored for future use, and data requiring further interpretation within RIFT.

(vii) **REFT processes information:** The Robotic Explanation Framework Toolkit (REFT) analyzes the received information and applies appropriate algorithms to derive explanations. Complex internal data are distilled into actionable insights that are understandable by human users.

(viii) **RIFT information stored in database:** To preserve generated insights, the system stores information produced by RIFT in a database. This repository supports the reuse of past interpretations and, in our implementation, is associated with a General Purpose Interpreter.

(ix) **Send information:** The synthesized explanations are transmitted to the Human–Machine Interface (HMI) output module. This step represents the culmination of the interpretability and explainability process, preparing the content for user presentation.

 (x) **Information presented to the user:** From different perspectives, and either with or without the full interpretive process completed, the system presents information to the user. Through visual displays, auditory cues, or textual summaries, the presentation is adapted to optimize user comprehension.

(xi) **Previous explanations inform data collection:** Finally, the system leverages previously generated explanations stored in the database to inform future data collection processes. By exploiting historical context, the system improves its capacity to anticipate user needs and refine its interpretive behavior.

4.3   Toolkit and Regulatory Compliance

In this study, we aim to integrate tools into the robotic architecture that not only enhance user understanding but also ensure compliance with the requirements of the EU AI Act. Table 1 maps ROXIE components to specific AI Act articles. This mapping illustrates how the proposed technical implementation directly supports regulatory compliance.

Table 1. AI Act compliance mapping.

AI Act Article	ROXIE Component	Implementation
Art. 13 (Transparency)	REFT	Natural language explanations, visual interfaces
Art. 14 (Human Oversight)	RIFT	Multi-level interpretability, user-adapted explanations
Art. 15 (Accuracy)	Model Interpreter	SHAP and LIME analysis tools
Art. 17 (Data Quality)	RAFT	Secure logging, data validation

Besides, Table 2 showcases the tools we currently utilize, mapped both to our framework requirements and to relevant state-of-the-art tools.

Table 2. Tools used at different stages of this research for explaining robot behaviors to end-users.

ROXIE Component	Req.	Tools	Cite
All	R0.1	ROS SealFS, immutable BBR	[23, 26]
All	R0.2	llama_ros, LLaMA	[5, 25]
All	R1.1	ROS 2	[15]
All	R1.2	GROOT, YASMIN viewer, Foxglove	[2, 4, 7]
All	R1.3	ROS 2	[15]
All	R2.1	YAML, `.config`, `.csv`, `.json`, launcher	N/A
All	R2.2	HuggingFace, YOLOv8	[8, 10]
All	R2.3	HuggingFace, YOLOv8	[8, 10]
All	R2.4	TEB Planner	[29]
REFT, RIFT	R3.1	SHAP, LIME, CAPTUM, LRP, easy_explain	[11, 14, 19, 24]
REFT, RIFT	R3.2	CAPTUM, ad-hoc methods	[11]
REFT	R4.1	LLaVA, Stable Diffusion	[13, 18]
RAFT	R5.1	EBB Winfield, AaaS	[3, 26, 28]

5   Conclusions

This paper has presented ROXIE, a requirements-driven framework for explainability, interpretability, and accountability in autonomous robotic systems. Rather than proposing a monolithic architecture or a specific implementation, ROXIE structures existing and emerging techniques into three complementary toolkits (REFT, RIFT, and RAFT), which are organized around clear functional and regulatory requirements. This approach responds to the growing need for systematic and transparent robotic systems operating in public and safety-relevant environments.

A key contribution of ROXIE lies in explicitly separating interpretability and explainability concerns while acknowledging their interdependence. Interpretability is addressed through mechanisms that expose internal decision-making processes and evidence sources, whereas explainability focuses on translating this information into intelligible, role-adaptive representations for different stakeholders. Accountability is treated as a first-class concern through durable, secure, and traceable recording mechanisms that support post-hoc analysis and regulatory compliance.

By aligning the framework with the EU Artificial Intelligence Act and complementary standards such as IEEE P7001 and ISO/IEC 42001:2023, this work positions explainability, interpretability, and cybersecurity not as optional features, but as foundational requirements for trustworthy autonomous robots. The proposed mappings between requirements, tools, and regulatory obligations illustrate how compliance considerations can be integrated directly into robotic system design.

The proof-of-concept scenario demonstrates how ROXIE can be instantiated using existing ROS 2 tools, highlighting its practical applicability while also revealing current limitations. In particular, this work does not claim empirical validation of performance, usability, or faithfulness of explanations, nor does it provide quantitative assessments of system overhead. These aspects are intentionally left for future work.

Future research will focus on validating ROXIE through empirical studies, including user-centered evaluations, performance measurements, and real-world deployments. Further efforts are also required to refine the interaction between large language models and accountability mechanisms, address the risks introduced by opaque explanation generators, and strengthen traceability between regulatory requirements and technical artifacts. Overall, ROXIE aims to serve as a common reference framework to guide the development of transparent, interpretable, and accountable robotic systems as regulatory and societal expectations continue to evolve.

Acknowledgments. Francisco J. Rodriguez Lera acknowledges support from Grant PID2021-126592OB-C21 and Grant PID2024-161761OB-C21, funded by MICIU/AEI/ 10.13039/501100011033 and by the ERDF/EU. The ULE team acknowledges support from Grant PID2024-162298OB-I00, funded by MICIU/AEI/10.13039/501100011033 and by the ERDF/EU. Irene González Fernández acknowledges support from the CORESENSE project, funded by the European Commission's Horizon Europe programme under Grant Agreement No. 101070254 (HORIZON-CL4-2021-DIGITAL-EMERGING-01-11).

The authors acknowledge the use of an AI-based language model to assist with English language revision and stylistic improvements. All scientific content, interpretations, and conclusions are the sole responsibility of the authors.

References

1. Anjomshoae, S., Najjar, A., Calvaresi,D., Främling, K.: Explainable agents and robots: Results from a systematic literature review. In: Proceedings of the 18th International Conference on Autonomous agents and MultiAgent Systems, AAMAS 2019, pp. 1078–1088 (2019)
2. BehaviorTree.CPP Developers, Groot: Graphical editor for BehaviorTree.CPP (2023). https://github.com/BehaviorTree/Groot
3. Fernández-Becerra, L., Guerrero-Higueras, Á.M., Rodríguez-Lera, F.J., Matellán, V.: Accountability as a service for robotics: performance assessment of different accountability strategies for autonomous robots. Logic J. IGPL **32**, 243–262 (2024)
4. Foxglove, Foxglove platform (2023). https://foxglove.dev
5. González-Santamarta, M. A.: LLaMA ROS (2023). https://github.com/mgonzs13/ llama_ros

6. González-Santamarta, M.A.: YOLOv8 ROS (2023). https://github.com/mgonzs13/yolov8_ros

7. González-Santamarta, M.Á., Rodríguez-Lera, F.J., Matellán-Olivera, V., Fernández-Llamas, C.: YASMIN: Yet another state machine. In: ROBOT2022: Fifth Iberian Robotics Conference, pp. 528–539 (2023)

8. Hugging Face, Hugging Face platform (2023). https://huggingface.co

9. International Organization for Standardization and International Electrotechnical Commission, ISO/IEC 42001:2023 – information technology – artificial intelligence – management system. https://www.iso.org/es/norma/42001 (2023). international Standard

10. Jocher, G. et al.: YOLO by Ultralytics (2023). https://github.com/ultralytics/ultralytics

11. Kokhlikyan, N., et al.: Captum: A unified and generic model interpretability library for pytorch (2020). https://arxiv.org/abs/2009.07896

12. Lewis, P., et al.: Retrieval-augmented generation for knowledge-intensive nlp tasks. In: Proceedings of the 34th International Conference on Neural Information Processing Systems, NIPS 2020 (2020)

13. Liu, H., Li, C., Li, Y, Lee, Y.J.: Improved baselines with visual instruction tuning (2024). https://arxiv.org/abs/2310.03744

14. Lundberg, S.M., Lee, S.-I.: A unified approach to interpreting model predictions. In: Proceedings of the 31st International Conference on Neural Information Processing Systems, NIPS 2017, pp. 4768–4777 (2017)

15. Macenski, S., Foote, T., Gerkey, B., Lalancette, C., Woodall, W.: Robot operating system 2: design, architecture, and uses in the wild. Sci. Robot. **7**, eabm6074 (2022)

16. Macenski, S., Martín, F., White, R., Clavero, J.G.: The marathon 2: a navigation system. In: 2020 IEEE/RSJ International Conference on Intelligent Robots and Systems (IROS), pp. 2718–2725 (2020)

17. Pennington, N., Hastie, R.: Reasoning in explanation-based decision making. Cognition **49**, 123–163 (1993). https://www.sciencedirect.com/science/article/pii/001002779390038W

18. Podell, D., et al.: Sdxl: improving latent diffusion models for high-resolution image synthesis (2023). https://arxiv.org/abs/2307.01952

19. Ribeiro, M.T., Singh, S., Guestrin, C.: Why Should I Trust You?: explaining the predictions of any classifier. In: Proceedings of the 22nd ACM SIGKDD International Conference on Knowledge Discovery and Data Mining, KDD 2016, pp. 1135–1144 (2016). https://doi.org/10.1145/2939672.2939778

20. Rudin, C.: Stop explaining black box machine learning models for high stakes decisions and use interpretable models instead. Nat. Mach. Intell. **1**, 206–215 (2019)

21. Sahoo, P., Singh, A.K., Saha, S., Jain, V., Mondal, S., Chadha, A.: A systematic survey of prompt engineering in large language models: techniques and applications (2025). https://arxiv.org/abs/2402.07927

22. Sobrín-Hidalgo, D., Santamarta, M.Á.G., Guerrero-Higueras, Á. M., Rodríguez-Lera, F.J., Olivera, V.M.: Explaining autonomy: Enhancing human–robot interaction through explanation generation with large language models, CoRR abs (2024). https://doi.org/10.48550/arXiv.2402.04206

23. Soriano-Salvador, E., Guardiola-Múzquiz, G.: Sealfs: storage-based tamper-evident logging. Comput. Sec. **108**, 102325 (2021). https://www.sciencedirect.com/science/article/pii/S0167404821001498

24. Theocharis, S.: *easy_explain* (2023). https://github.com/stavrostheocharis/easy_explain

25. Touvron, H., et al.: Llama 2: Open foundation and fine-tuned chat models (2023). https://arxiv.org/abs/2307.09288
26. White, R., Caiazza, G., Cortesi, A., Cho, Y.I., Christensen, H.I.: Black block recorder: immutable black box logging for robots via blockchain. IEEE Robot. Autom. Lett. **4**, 3812–3819 (2019)
27. Winfield, A. F.T., et al.: IEEE P7001: A proposed standard on transparency. Front. Robot. AI **8**(2021) (2021). https://www.frontiersin.org/journals/robotics-and-ai/articles/10.3389/frobt.2021.665729
28. Winfield, A. F.T., van Maris, A., Salvini, P., Jirotka, M.: An ethical black box for social robots: a draft open standard (2022). https://arxiv.org/abs/2205.06564
29. Wu, J., Ma, X., Peng, T., Wang, H.: An improved timed elastic band (teb) algorithm of autonomous ground vehicle (agv) in complex environment. Sensors **21** (2021). https://www.mdpi.com/1424-8220/21/24/8312

Augmenting an LLM-Based Tutor Agent with a Large Action Model for Multimodal Interaction

Piotr Kluczyński[1]([✉]), Arthur Picard[2] , Yazan Mualla[2] , Hedi Tebourbi[3] , Sana Nouzri[3] , Abdeljalil Abbas-Turki[2] , and Franck Gechter[2]

[1] Bialystok University of Technology, Wiejska 45A, 15-351 Bialystok, Poland
`89285@student.pb.edu.pl`
[2] Université de Technologie de Belfort Montbéliard, UTBM, CIAD UR 7533, 90010 Belfort, France
[3] University of Luxembourg, 4365 Esch-sur-Alzette, Luxembourg

Abstract. The rapid adoption of Large Language Models (LLMs) is transforming diverse sectors, including education, by enabling personalized learning experiences. Artificial Intelligence (AI) agents support adaptive instruction, instant feedback, automated assessment, and content generation, enhancing access to individualized resources. However, current systems often lack accuracy and offer limited HumanâĂŞAgent Interaction (HAI), a key factor in effective student engagement. To address this, we propose a visual interaction mechanism that augments chatbot communication with image-based responses. We extend an LLM-powered tutor agent by incorporating a Large Action Model (LAM), enabling the agent to execute image-based functions alongside text generation. Building on a LangGraph-orchestrated prototype, we developed two LAM-integrated tools: 1) an Image Retrieval Tool that accesses a vector database of textbook illustrations, and 2) an Image Cropping Tool that dynamically extracts regions from textbook pages. These were implemented using OpenAI's Function Calling API and evaluated with the GPT-4o mini model. In controlled trials on single textbook pages, the Image Retrieval Tool consistently identifies relevant illustrations, while the Cropping Tool frequently returns visually plausible but pedagogically irrelevant regions. This reveals a precisionâĂŞflexibility trade-off: curated retrieval ensures accuracy, whereas dynamic cropping offers broader applicability at the expense of reduced relevance. We also identify challenges in synchronizing tool calls with textual explanations and scaling manual dataset preparation. Our results suggest that LAM-enhanced function-calling can significantly improve HAI in educational contexts, highlighting directions for automating content curation and enhancing interaction consistency.

Keywords: LLMs · LAMs · Personalized Adaptive Learning · Language Learning · RAG · Generative Pre-trained Transformer

© The Author(s), under exclusive license to Springer Nature Switzerland AG 2026
Y. Mualla et al. (Eds.): CALM 2025, CCIS 2923, pp. 31–46, 2026.
https://doi.org/10.1007/978-3-032-20548-3_3

1   Introduction

Generative Artificial Intelligence (GenAI) and Large Language Models (LLMs) are now part of daily life. Their most familiar form is the chatbot, a model that generates text to converse with humans. Their uses range from online consultants to writers, but one of their most promising applications is education. Research on automated learning focuses on robot tutors designed to support students during self-directed study.

AI has significantly reshaped personalized learning, with adaptive learning technologies playing a central role [10,27,34]. These systems tailor educational content and interactions to individual student performance and pace [11,28, 33]. Traditional methods often lack such personalization, prompting the rise of Intelligent Tutoring Systems, which improve learning through advanced Human-Agent Interaction (HAI). It is increasingly recognized that fostering effective communication and understanding between humans and AI systems is vital for their successful integration into various applications [17,18].

As demonstrated by Nouzri et al. [19], the use of a single LLM-based chatbot has limited capabilities to provide an effective learning experience for students. To mitigate this, they employed an LLM-based Multi-Agent System (MAS) and divided the various language learning challenges among the agents. In this way, each agent was able to focus on one aspect of the language, rather than trying to grasp its full complexity. In addition, to increase the accuracy and fidelity of the models, a Retrieval-Augmented Generation (RAG) system was built, based on language learning textbooks published by the National Institute of Languages of Luxembourg [9]. The system by Tebourbi et al. [6,7,31] improves HAI by delegating language tasks to multiple specialized agents. This approach, while providing a high level of interaction between the user and the overall system, does not improve the HAI for individual chatbots, which are still restricted to using text-only responses.

Indeed, the use of visual information enhances the exchange between AI and the user by activating additional memorization pathways, particularly those linked to visual memory, thereby reinforcing understanding and retention [14]. Moreover, the integration of AI into wearable devices such as AI/XR headsets or AI/HUD (Head-up display) glasses increases the need for multimodal HAI inter-action to ensure a clearer understanding—offering. This multi-modal interaction thus brings a valuable perspective on AI explainability.

This paper aims to explore potential ways to improve HAI during conversations by developing a chatbot based on the Large Action Model (LAM) [35]. Using OpenAI's Function Calling API [4], we enable the chatbot to embed images in its replies, making the dialogue more interactive for students.

The rest of the article is structured as follows: Sect. 2 analyzes the current use of LLM in the field of learning, then Sect. 3 presents an already existing system for learning Luxembourgish. Section 4 describes our methodology for the developed solutions. In Sect. 5, we explain the implementation of the provided solutions, after which we describe the results of our work in Sect. 6. Section 8 concludes the article and highlights potential future directions.

2 Related Work

2.1 Large Language Models in Learning

Since LLMs have achieved student-level performance when dealing with academic challenges, their use in the field of learning has become very common [32]. Moreover, while chatbots equipped with universal knowledge, such as ChatGPT, can solve and provide answers to even very complex challenges, there are a large number of specialized tools and techniques designed to support the learning process [29].

One of the most basic skills needed to master a language is the ability to form correct sentences. Experiments by Zhang et al. [36] show that the use of few-shot learning practice allows LLMs to achieve extremely high efficiency in error correcting on very challenging problems such as Chinese Text Correction and English Grammar Correction. This is of great importance because LLMs with such abilities can help students learn this key skill without the help of a teacher.

The generative capabilities of LLMs are also being used to enhance learning by personalizing the educational experience to the student's abilities [32]. Such an application has been explored in the Taiwan Adaptive Learning Platform [12], where LLM has been implemented to generate personalized learning paths, tailored to the user's performance. The use of LLM models in assessing students' skills is of great importance as it allows the system to expand questions on a given topic beyond multiple-choice questions and replace them with open-ended questions, allowing it to better understand student problems.

The application of LLM models in education is not limited to supporting students; these models are also used by teachers themselves, enabling them to perform their work more effectively [2,15,24]. A good example of such use of LLM is the *gotLearning* platform, which not only provides personalised assessments to students using the *gotFeedback* application, but also supports their mentors by generating an analysis of student learning outcomes, helping them to identify potential weaknesses in students' understanding of the material. As the use of LLMs shows strong justification and finds increasingly more use cases, this is an area of continuous research, with many different directions being explored.

2.2 Large Action Models

Large Action Models are new, but early prototypes already show promise for education. The best-known example of automating typical user activity on a computer is the OpenAI Operator agent [22]. This Computer-Using Agent is trained to interact with graphical user interfaces (GUIs) by continuously taking GUI screenshots as input and performing actions, such as clicking, scrolling, or typing. Moreover, it has high reasoning capabilities, utilizing a chain-of-thought to break down complex tasks into an action plan, which it then proceeds to execute [20]. While this use of LAM does not provide a direct way to enhance learning, it shows the ingenuity and capability of the LAM approach.

LAMs are also used in commercial electrical equipment, such as the Rabbit R1 [25]. The latter is a small smartphone-like device equipped with an AI agent capable of variety of performing various functions. In addition to operator-like abilities (browsing the web, searching for information, etc.), the agent can mimic the actions presented to it. Using the learning mode function, the user can record the process of performing any action, which the agent then learns to perform in the future. This device [25] is an excellent example of a useful application of LAM and demonstrates the capabilities of universal agents capable of dynamically learning their tasks.

Despite the great interest in the topic of LAMs and their possible application in the field of education, there are, according to our knowledge, no systems that fully exploit the capabilities of LAMs to improve learning. Nevertheless, the technology is the subject of ongoing research [21,26], and its use in the field seems to be only a matter of time.

2.3   Language Learning Applications

Because of the complexity of the language learning process, a single LLM is rarely responsible for this task; although the solution is still implemented in the application, it is a component of the entire system.

Duolingo leverages LLMs for conversational practice and for exercise generation. In particular, Duolingo Max uses GPT-4 to create and adapt learning content under human supervision, illustrating a real-world deployment of LLMs for language-learning material generation [3].

Talkpal takes a more direct approach: it offers several chatbot-based tools to learn a language [30]. During various conversations with the LLM agent, the application emphasizes the continuous feedback, in the form of grammar corrections and regular grammar advice summaries, sent through email. The functionalities of this application, while very basic, tap into the potential of LLMs to provide user with not only the correct answer, but also the explanation of their mistakes.

Another use of LLMs goes beyond teaching the user the grammar rules and vocabulary of the language and introduces them to the culture of the corresponding nation. The experiment of Mageira et al. introduces the AsasaraBot, a tutoring chatbot, which was supposed to complement the courses taught in foreign languages [16]. While the study highlighted that such a system would not be able to fully replace the human tutor, it highlighted a positive impact on the learning process for both student and teacher.

3   Pre-built Demo Overview

The most significant work-in-progress, exploring the possibilities of LLM in education, is the *Luxembourgish Tutoring Chatbot*, a language learning application, currently existing in a demo version. The demo showcases a fully functional Multi-Agent System for personalized Luxembourgish learning [7,19], built on a Python/FastAPI backend and a React frontend. Agent workflows are orchestrated via LangGraph [13] (an extension of LangChain [5]), which manages stateful communication between:

- **Communicator Agent**, responsible for user authentication, preference retrieval, and progress review
- **Orchestrator Agent**, which fetches and validates instructional content (via RAG) before sequencing it into coherent lessons
- **Tracker Agent**, monitoring user interactions and coordinating task hand-offs among agents
- **Tutor Agents**, a suite of specialized tutor agents covering conversation practice, reading exercises, listening comprehension, grammar summaries, and Questions & Answers drills.

The React interface provides learners with intuitive dashboards for lesson selection, progress visualization, and real-time agent dialogue, while a Text-To-Speech component delivers audio prompts and feedback. User data, such as completed topics and performance metrics, is stored securely, enabling the system to adapt future sessions to each learner's strengths and weaknesses (see Fig. 1).

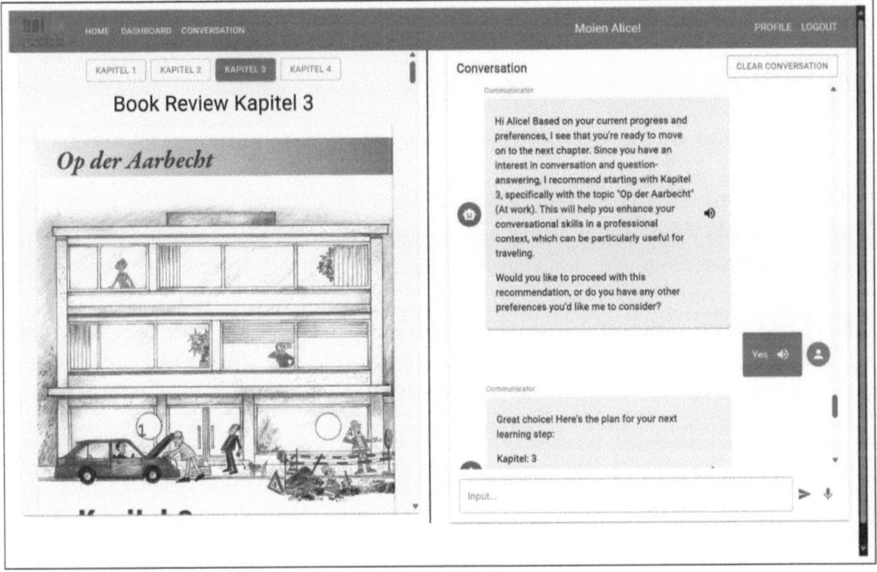

Fig. 1. Current chat interface. The left-hand panel displays static textbook images; the LAM-enhanced tool in Sect. 4 lets the LLM choose exercises and images dynamically and render them here.

In a typical demo scenario, a returning learner "John" logs in and is greeted by the *Communicator Agent* with options to review his last session or advance to the next topic. Choosing to proceed, the *Orchestrator Agent* immediately retrieves the tailored materials for Topic 2 of Kapitel 1. The *Tracker Agent* then sequences two targeted activities, an interactive dialogue exercise from the *Conversational Agent* and a listening comprehension task from the *Listening Agent*, providing instant feedback and logging results. Once completed, John's profile is updated and the *Communicator Agent* summarizes his achievements and recommends next steps, illustrating the end-to-end adaptive learning flow.

Although the demo version of the application already makes extensive use of LLMs and places a strong emphasis on HAI, its current design still leaves room for improving the core interaction between the conversational agent and the learner, which we explore in the next section. Currently, the left-hand panel of the chat interface displays only static, pre-selected illustrations; the new LAM-based tool described in this paper empowers the LLM to dynamically choose the most relevant exercise and fetch context-appropriate images, rendering them in that same panel to enrich the dialogue in real time.

4   Methodology

To seamlessly integrate imagery into educational dialogues and move beyond "text-only" responses, the tutor agent needs an LAM that can both acquire images and surface them during dialogue.

Glossary. For clarity, we summarize the key terms used throughout the paper:

- **LLM (Large Language Model)** âĂŞ the GPT-4o mini model accessed via the OpenAI API.
- **Tutor agent** âĂŞ the conversational component that wraps the LLM, manages prompts, and issues tool calls.
- **Application** âĂŞ the complete demo platform (backend services, vector store, tools, and React-based UI).
- **LAM (Large Action Model)** âĂŞ an action-execution framework enabling the agent to call tools (e.g., retrieve or crop images) during dialogue.
- **RAG (Retrieval-Augmented Generation)** âĂŞ a mechanism that fetches curated textbook content to ground the LLM's responses.

LAM is essential for strengthening HAI because it empowers LLMs to do more than just generate text: they can execute retrieval calls, embed visuals, and orchestrate multimodal content in real time. In this paper, we compare two distinct LAM–powered architectures, each offering a different balance of autonomy and control: one limits the selection of images to a pre-selected set, while the other allows the model to independently select content from the textbook page. By examining their trade–offs, we show how a well–designed LAM can turn a conversational agent into a true multimodal tutor.

The first solution, *Image Retrieval Tool,* is very restrictive: it only allows pre-selected illustrations from the textbook. This approach is based on the RAG system, which is used to build a vector database of images. During testing the LLM was able to retrieve an image matching the ongoing topic.

The second solution, *Image Cropping Tool*, provides more freedom in the selection of images to be used during the conversation. It provides the tutor agent with the ability to provide coordinates inside the currently worked on page from the textbook, according to which the system will retrieve a portion of the image and incorporate it into the conversation with the student.

The scripts and resources used in developing both tools are available in GitHub repositories: Image Retrieval Tool[1], Image Cropping Tool[2].

As the technical limitations of LLMs are overcome, more companies are increasingly choosing to implement AI in their learning support tools, so the process of developing such applications is dynamic and ongoing.

4.1   Image Retrieval Tool

When the tutor agent decides to use the tool, it returns the corresponding call in a response message. Along with the call itself, the tutor agent provides a textual description of the image and the meta-parameters describing it: topic name, page, and chapter number. When the application backend detects a tool call in the agent response, it retrieves the parameter values and accesses a previously created vector store to find the best-matching image. Image identification is done by binary matching all meta-parameters and comparing text-description embeddings with image embeddings. Once the best match is identified, the application backend retrieves its identification number and accesses the corresponding image from a separate database. The image is then returned to the user together with the agent-generated text response. The workflow of the Image Retrieval Tool is shown in Fig. 2.

In order for the Image Retrieval Tool to work, an image dataset needs to be selected and a vector store containing its embeddings needs to be created. According to our design, all images should be extracted from a certified textbook to ensure their relevance to student learning. Each image should be embedded using a multi-modal embedding function. In addition, each embed is stored in a vector store along with meta-parameters: topic name, page number, and chapter number, describing the part of the textbook from which the image was extracted. A mapping between the stored images and their embeddings is then created to facilitate the search for relevant images.

Although the general idea of a dataset was developed, both image extraction and the creation of the vector store were done manually, due to the experimental version of the tools. Moreover, to enhance the capability of the LLM to properly use the provided tool, alongside the user message, the LLM receives the image of the textbook page as input.

---

[1] https://github.com/piotr-kluczynski/image-retrieval.
[2] https://github.com/piotr-kluczynski/image-cropping.

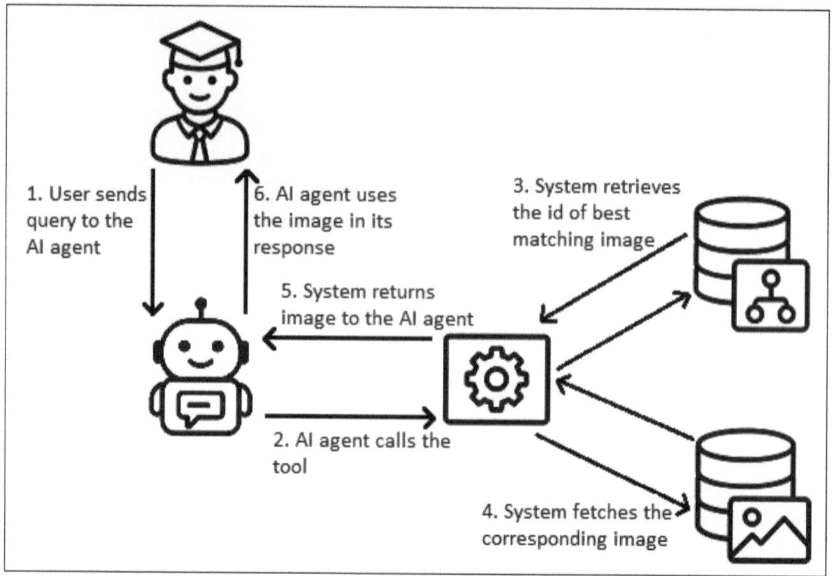

Fig. 2. Schematic of Image Retrieval Tool workflow.

4.2   Image Cropping Tool

During the call, the LLM receives an image of the textbook page the student is currently working on and its dimensions. When the proposed AI agent decides to use the Image Cropping tool, it sends the appropriate call, with four numbers (representing the x and y positions of the top-left and bottom-right points, respectively) as arguments in the response. The application backend detects the tool call and retrieves the coordinates of the top-left and bottom-right corners of the box. The rectangle formed by these coordinates is then cropped from the textbook page currently under development and appended to the LLM's text response in a message to the user. The workflow of the Image Cropping Tool is shown in the diagram in Fig. 3.

To increase the capability of the LLM to properly use this tool, the LLM receives the image of the textbook page and its dimensions as input.

5   Integrating Proposed Tools Into the Pre-Built Demo

To facilitate integration with an existing OpenAI-powered agent system, both image-centric tools were implemented in Python using the official OpenAI client library. The core image-processing routines leverage OpenCV [23] for pixel-level operations and ChromaDB [1] to organize and query image embeddings in a vector database.

The temporary Chroma DB collection, created for purposes of this experiment, used the Contrastive Language-Image Pre-training (CLIP) as its embedding model, specifically the open-source OpenCLIP [8] implementation. By

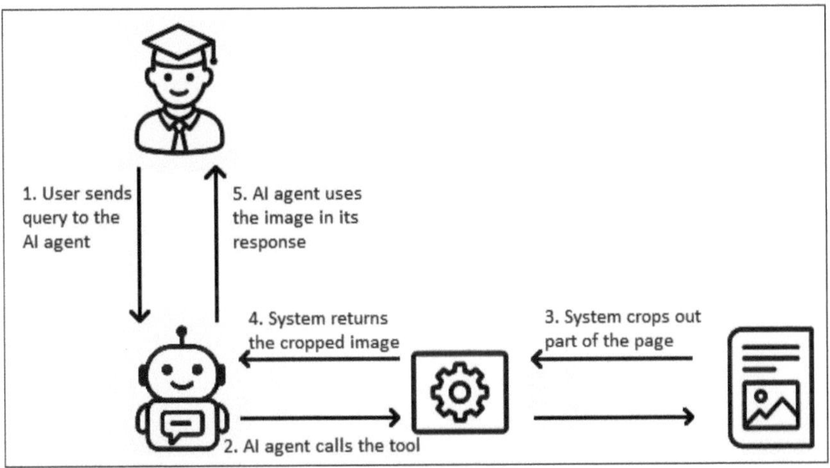

Fig. 3. Schematic of Image Cropping Tool workflow.

adopting this solution, the collection was capable of embedding text and images alike, allowing similarity checks between text and images. The comparison between embeddings was performed using Euclidean (L2) distance.

Each tool is exposed to the Large Language Model via OpenAI's Function Calling interface, allowing the LLM to invoke "retrieve-image" or "crop-image"" operations as if they were native API methods. This seamless binding ensures that, once the LLM emits a function call, our backend intercepts it, executes the requested action, and returns the result to the conversation.

To guide the LLM toward correct usage, we supplied curated examples alongside each tool definition: one illustrative prompt/response pair for the Image Retrieval Tool and two for the Image Cropping Tool. Each example comprises the user's query, the ideal textual reply, and the precise function invocation. Those examples of proper use of the tool are sent in the application's system prompts to shape the LLM's behavior and reduce the number of miscalls.

6   Results

We evaluated the Image Retrieval Tool by extracting a single page from the textbook, isolating four images to construct a vector store, and initializing a temporary collection with ChromaDB. The Image Cropping Tool was similarly tested using another, manually selected page from the textbook. In both cases, we employed the GPT-4o mini model via the OpenAI API. To isolate and assess each tool's effectiveness, we activated a flag that forced the LLM to invoke the designated tool in its responses. Both textbook pages used in tools evaluation are shown in the Fig. 4).

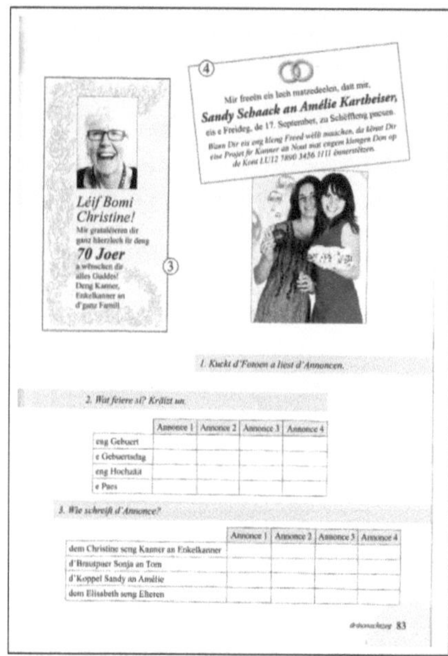

(a) Example for Image Retrieval Tool

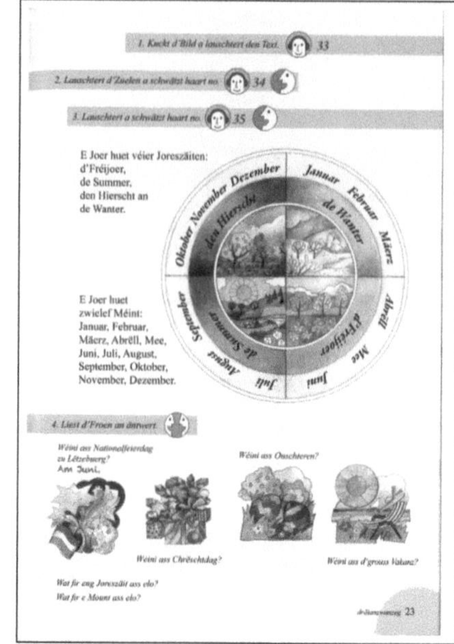

(b) Example for Image Cropping Tool

Fig. 4. Example images provided to the tools.

6.1   Image Retrieval Tool Results

We manually extracted the images (a), (b), (c), and (d) in Fig. 5 from the example image (Fig. 4,(a)) to create a test dataset.

The LLM was provided with an example of a correct interaction with the user and then received a new, previously unseen image of a textbook page together with a prompt simulating the user's question: "I am currently working on the second exercise 'Wat feire si? Kraizt un.', but I have a problem determining what kind of announcement number 4 represents. Provide me with both a textual explanation and the image I am describing."

Upon receiving the user call, the LLM correctly returned the Image Retrieval Tool call with all parameters (text description of the image to be retrieved, chapter number, topic name, and page number where the image is located), but did not return any text response accompanying the function call. When the function call was intercepted, the application backend matched the provided parameters with the sub-image (d) in Fig. 4 and retrieved it from the collection.

Although the retrieved image d (from Fig. 5) accurately depicted the relevant part of the page, it contained only a photograph of two women, unlike sub-image b (from Fig. 5), which included all the information related to announcement 4. Given the general nature of the user's question, we would have expected sub-image b to be selected; therefore, the answer could be considered only partially correct.

(a)

(b)

(c)

(d)

Fig. 5. Sub-images extracted from the textbook page.

6.2   Image Cropping Tool Results

The LLM was provided with two examples of a correct tool call, a new textbook
page to extract images from, and a system message explaining its task: "You
will be provided with an image of a textbook page for learning Luxembourgish
and the dimensions of the image (Width, Height). Your task is to analyze it and
decide whether there are parts of the image (pictures, drawings, etc.) that could
be useful during the Luxembourgish learning process. If you identify a relevant
part of the image, call the crop_image tool with the correct parameters (x and y

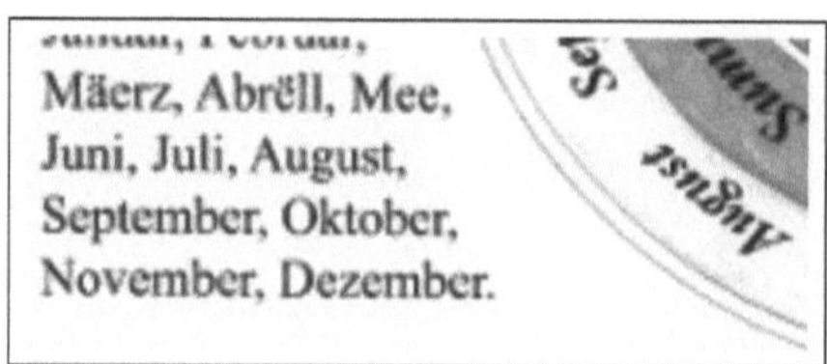

Fig. 6. First sub-image obtained using Image Cropping Tool.

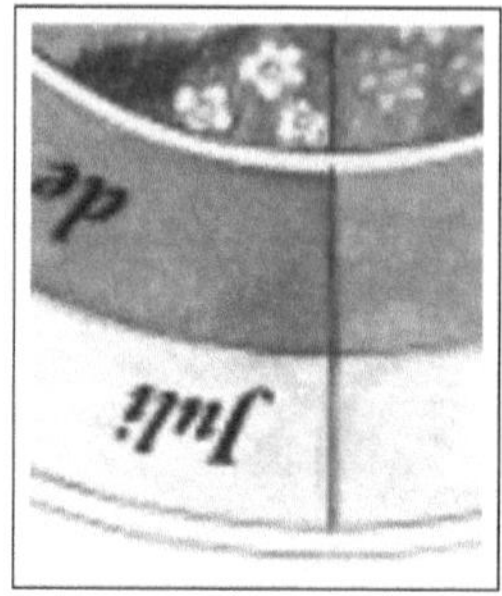

Fig. 7. Second sub-image obtained using Image Cropping Tool.

positions of the top-left and bottom-right points). In the response, explain your decision."

The LLM response, although it contained two valid tool calls with the correct locations on the image of the textbook page, did not include an accompanying text response.

When the tool call was detected, the application backend cropped part of the image according to the coordinates provided by the LLM. The resulting sub-images shown in Figs. 6 and 7 presented incomplete parts of the textbook page that were insignificant and did not contain any meaningful elements; therefore, the result must be considered entirely incorrect.

7   Comparison and Discussion

Although the limited scope of the test conducted makes it impossible to give a definitive verdict on the effectiveness of the tools created, the results provide some insight into the possibilities and challenges of the approaches used.

A direct comparison of the results obtained using both tools clearly shows the advantage of the Image Retrieval Tool over the Image Cropping Tool. Although the sub-image obtained with the Image Retrieval Tool was not the best possible match among all options, it was extremely similar to the expected one, indicating that this issue was of little importance. Furthermore, the results of the Image Retrieval Tool are significantly better than the two sub-images cropped using the Image Cropping Tool, which had no educational value and were useless in the teaching process.

Although when comparing these two solutions, the Image Retrieval Tool is the clear winner, its results are not entirely correct, as the images retrieved from the database only partially match the image description requested by the user. While this problem seems relatively serious, there is a potential explanation for this error: nearly identical images in the prepared set. Since the matching process relies on finding the smallest L2 distance between the embedding of a given description and the embeddings of images from the vector store, in the case of very similar, partially overlapping images, it can be difficult to retrieve a specific image. Our example seems to confirm this theory âĂŞ images b and d (Fig. 5) shared a significant portion of their content, so the description returned by the LLM was not the one it needed. Nevertheless, although this explanation is convincing, more detailed tests need to be carried out to clarify the matter.

The initial success of the Image Retrieval Tool calls for it to be further developed and incorporated into the application currently under development. However, in order to implement this tool into the pre-built demo application, the problem of its scalability needs to be solved. To develop and test the tool, we used hand-cut images from a single page of the textbook, but doing this for each page would require an alarming amount of time to prepare the image database, and is not optimal in the long run.

Although the failure of the Image Cropping Tool is obvious, its causes are not. A potential cause could be the inability of the LLM to return a numerical value indicating the position of an area in the image. Being an LLM, working on numbers without access to external tools can be quite a challenge, especially when the need for computation is not obvious. Another reason for the application backend's failure can be the sheer challenge of analyzing the resulting image for relevant parts that should be cropped out. Both the definition of important parts, given to the LLM, and their location in the image may have been key factors in the failure of this approach.

It is also worth noting the potential limitations of the OpenAI LLM in terms of maintaining conversational continuity and using Function Calling. When testing the developed tools, the tested LLMs had great difficulty in simultaneously returning a valuable textual response intended for the user and calling for the tool. This may result in a degradation of HAI effectiveness and decline in overall user-experience quality.

Although the focus of this work is on the image extraction process itself, it is worth considering whether the selection of images (i.e., illustrations from the textbook pages) used to create the dataset for the Image Retrieval Tool is correct. If the tool being developed aims to improve HAI, the existing selection of images based on drawings from the textbook may be unnecessary for the users themselves during the learning process. Therefore, it may be valuable to identify what visual content might be helpful to the student during the conversation.

8   Conclusion and Future Work

This paper explores how existing chatbot solutions can be extended with LAM features to improve HAI during conversations with users. Using two different approaches, we demonstrated how an LLM-based chatbot could become a more effective teacher. While we have performed our work thoroughly, some aspects need further improvement.

The testing phase in our experiment was carried out on a minimal test sample and is not sufficient to clearly identify the right tool or to fully assess its actual effectiveness. Furthermore, the current configuration of parameters, such as the LLM using the tools, the initial message explaining the task set for the LLM, was chosen based on personal observations, and it is uncertain whether these are the best possible options. For these reasons, one possible solution is to conduct a larger-scale experiment on both (or one) tools.

Nevertheless, the insights provided by our experiment allow us to assume that the Image Retrieval Tool is a potential solution to our problem of improving HAI during chatbot conversations. Therefore, further development of this tool and its implementation into a full system is an equally important direction of future work. A practical next step is enabling the LLM to generate both its textual explanation and the tool call in the same turn. A system that fixes this weakness could, for example, resend a query to the model after detecting a tool call to add a text response accompanying the selected image before the image is sent to the user.

In addition, future work should address the Image Retrieval Tool's dependence on a pre-prepared image database. As it would be a monotonous task to prepare such a dataset by hand, consideration should be given to the development of a tool that would enable to automate the extraction of relevant images from the textbook pages. The creation of such a tool would not only reduce the amount of tedious work involved but would also increase the application's versatility, which could be used to teach languages other than Luxembourgish, as valuable images would be retrieved from the textbook, serving as a knowledge base in an automated manner.

References

1. ChromaDB: Chromadb. https://www.trychroma.com/home, Accessed 11 Dec 2025
2. Doughty, J., et al.: A comparative study of ai-generated (GPT-4) and human-crafted mcqs in programming education. In: Herbert, N., Seton, C. (eds.) Proceedings of the 26th Australasian Computing Education Conference, ACE 2024, Sydney, NSW, Australia, 29 January 2024- 2 February 2024. pp. 114–123. ACM (2024). https://doi.org/10.1145/3636243.3636256
3. Duolingo: Duolingo max uses gpt-4 for new learning features (2023). https://blog.duolingo.com/duolingo-max Accessed 11 Dec 2025
4. Eleti, A., Harris, J., Kilpatrick, L.: Function calling and other api updates (2023). https://openai.com/index/function-calling-and-other-api-updates/ Accessed 11 Dec 2025
5. Elovic, A.: How to build the ultimate ai automation with multi-agent collaboration (2024). https://blog.langchain.com/how-to-build-the-ultimate-ai-automation-with-multi-agent-collaboration Accessed 11 Dec 2025
6. Hedi, T., Nouzri, S., Mualla, Y., Abbas-Turki, A.: Artificial intelligence agents for personalized adaptive learning. Proc. Comput. Sci. **265**, 252–259 (2025)

7. Hedi, T., Nouzri, S., Mualla, Y., Najjar, A.: Personalized language learning: a multi-agent system leveraging llms for teaching luxembourgish. In: Das, S., Nowé, A., Vorobeychik, Y. (eds.) Proceedings of the 24th International Conference on Autonomous Agents and Multiagent Systems, AAMAS 2025, Detroit, MI, USA, May 19-23, 2025, pp. 3032–3034. International Foundation for Autonomous Agents and Multiagent Systems/ACM (2025).https://doi.org/10.5555/3709347.3744082

8. Ilharco, G., et al.: Openclip (2021). https://doi.org/10.5281/zenodo.5143773

9. Institut national des langues (INL): Schwätzt dir lëtzebuergesch? – niveau a1. Editions 2017/2018/2020/2021, Luxembourg (2021). https://sdl.inll.lu/book-a1-2017-2018-2020-2021/, Accessed 11 Dec 2025

10. Jian, M.J.K.O.: Personalized learning through ai. Adv. Eng. Innovation **5**, 16–19 (2023)

11. Kim, W., Kim, J.: Individualized AI tutor based on developmental learning networks. IEEE Access **8**, 27927–27937 (2020)

12. Kuo, B.C., Chang, F.T., Bai, Z.E.: Leveraging llms for adaptive testing and learning in taiwan adaptive learning platform (talp). In: LLM@ AIED, pp. 101–110 (2023)

13. LangChain: Langgraph: Multi-agent workflows. https://blog.langchain.com/langgraph-multi-agent-workflows (2024), Accessed 11 Dec 2025

14. Lazaro, M.J.S., Kim, S.: Review of multimodal interaction in optical see-through augmented reality. Int. J. Hum. Comput. Interact. **41**(17), 11227–11243 (2025). https://doi.org/10.1080/10447318.2024.2442128

15. Leiker, D., Finnigan, S., Gyllen, A.R., Cukurova, M.: Prototyping the use of large language models (llms) for adult learning content creation at scale. In: Moore, S., et al. (eds.) Proceedings of the Workshop on Empowering Education with LLMs - the Next-Gen Interface and Content Generation 2023 co-located with 24th International Conference on Artificial Intelligence in Education (AIED 2023), Tokyo, Japan, 7 July 7 2023. CEUR Workshop Proceedings, vol. 3487, pp. 3–7. CEUR-WS.org (2023), https://ceur-ws.org/Vol-3487/short1.pdf

16. Mageira, K., Pittou, D., Papasalouros, A., Kotis, K., Zangogianni, P., Daradoumis, A.: Educational ai chatbots for content and language integrated learning. Appl. Sci. **12**(7), 3239 (2022)

17. Mualla, Y.: Explaining the behavior of remote robots to humans: an agent-based approach. Ph.D. thesis, Université Bourgogne Franche-Comté (2020)

18. Mualla, Y., et al.: The quest of parsimonious XAI: A human-agent architecture for explanation formulation. Artif. Intell. **302**, 103573 (2022). https://doi.org/10.1016/J.ARTINT.2021.103573

19. Nouzri, S., Fatimi, M.E., Guerin, T., Othmane, M., Najjar, A.: Beyond chatbots: enhancing luxembourgish language learning through multi-agent systems and large language model. In: Arisaka, R., Sánchez-Anguix, V., Stein, S., Aydogan, R., van der Torre, L., Ito, T. (eds.) PRIMA 2024: Principles and Practice of Multi-Agent Systems - 25th International Conference, Kyoto, Japan, 18–24 November 2024, Proceedings. LNCS, vol. 15395, pp. 385–401. Springer (2024).https://doi.org/10.1007/978-3-031-77367-9_29

20. OpenAI: Computer-using agent: Introducing a universal interface for ai to interact with the digital world. https://openai.com/index/computer-using-agent (2025), Accessed 11 Dec 2025

21. OpenAI: Introducing chatgpt agent: bridging research and action. https://openai.com/index/introducing-chatgpt-agent (2025), Accessed 11 Dec 2025

22. OpenAI: Introducing operator. https://openai.com/index/introducing-operator (2025). Accessed 11 Dec 2025

23. OpenCV: Opencv. https://opencv.org, Accessed 11 Dec 2025
24. Pinto, G., Cardoso-Pereira, I., Monteiro, D., Lucena, D., de Souza, A.L.O.T., Gama, K.: Large language models for education: grading open-ended questions using chatgpt. In: Proceedings of the XXXVII Brazilian Symposium on Software Engineering, SBES 2023, Campo Grande, Brazil, 25-29 September 2023. pp. 293–302. ACM (2023). https://doi.org/10.1145/3613372.3614197
25. Rabbit Inc.: introducing r1, a pocket companion that moves ai from words to action (2024). https://www.rabbit.tech/newsroom/introducing-r1 Accessed 11 Dec 2025
26. Rabbit Inc.: rabbit officially launches its second product – rabbit intern. https://www.rabbit.tech/newsroom/rabbit-intern-launch (2025), Accessed 11 Dec 2025
27. Rızvı, M.: Investigating ai-powered tutoring systems that adapt to individual student needs, providing personalized guidance and assessments. Eurasia Proc. Educ. Soc. Sci. **31**, 67–73 (2023)
28. Sumak, B., Podgorelec, V., Karakatic, S., Dolenc, K., Sorgo, A.: Development of an autonomous, intelligent and adaptive e-learning system. In: Koricic, M., et al.(eds.) 42nd International Convention on Information and Communication Technology, Electronics and Microelectronics, MIPRO 2019, Opatija, Croatia, May 20-24, 2019. pp. 1492–1497. IEEE (2019). https://doi.org/10.23919/MIPRO.2019.8756889
29. Sumbal, A., Sumbal, R., Amir, A.: Can chatgpt-3.5 pass a medical exam? a systematic review of chatgpt's performance in academic testing. J. Med. Educ. Curricular Developm. **11**, 23821205241238641 (2024)
30. TalkPal: Talkpal. https://talkpal.ai, Accessed 11 Dec 2025
31. Tebourbi, H., et al.: Bpmn-based design of multi-agent systems: personalized language learning workflow automation with rag-enhanced knowledge access. Information **16**(9), 809 (2025)
32. Wang, S., et al.: Large language models for education: A survey and outlook. CoRR (2024). https://doi.org/10.48550/ARXIV.2403.18105
33. Xiao, J., Bai, Q.: itutor: promoting ai guided knowledge interaction in online learning. In: 2022 International Symposium on Educational Technology (ISET), pp. 253–257. IEEE (2022)
34. Xu, D., Wang, H.: Intelligent agent supported personalization for virtual learning environments. Decis. Support Syst. **42**(2), 825–843 (2006)
35. Zhang, J., et al.: xlam: a family of large action models to empower AI agent systems. CoRR (2024). https://doi.org/10.48550/ARXIV.2409.03215
36. Zhang, X., Zhang, X., Yang, C., Yan, H., Qiu, X.: Does correction remain a problem for large language models? CoRR (2023).https://doi.org/10.48550/ARXIV.2308.01776

Does the Model Say What the Data Says?
A Simple Heuristic for Model–Data Alignment

Henry Salgado[1]([✉]) [iD], Meagan R. Kendall[2] [iD], and Martine Ceberio[1] [iD]

[1] Department of Computer Science, The University of Texas at El Paso, El Paso, TX, USA
hsalgado@miners.utep.edu
[2] Department of Engineering Education and Leadership, The University of Texas at El Paso, El Paso, TX, USA

Abstract. In this work, we propose a simple, computationally efficient framework to evaluate whether machine learning models align with the structure of the data they learn from, that is, whether *the model says what the data says*. Unlike existing interpretability methods that focus exclusively on explaining model behavior, our approach establishes a baseline derived directly from the data itself. Drawing inspiration from Rubin's Potential Outcomes Framework, we measure how strongly each feature separates two outcome groups in a binary classification task, going beyond traditional descriptive statistics to quantify each feature's effect on the outcome. By comparing these data-derived feature rankings against model-based explanations, we provide practitioners with an interpretable method to assess model–data alignment.

Keywords: Causality · Interpretability · Data Fidelity

1 Introduction

As Deep Learning models grow in power and complexity, they have also become increasingly opaque. For example, modern architectures such as those used by Large Language Models (LLMs) often contain billions or even trillions of parameters, effectively turning them into "black boxes" whose internal mappings between weights and decisions are largely uninterpretable to humans [1]. This lack of transparency poses serious challenges in high-stakes domains where understanding model reasoning is critical in establishing trust, accountability, and fairness [2].

The consequences of this interpretability gap are already evident across multiple application areas. In healthcare, image-based diagnostic systems have been shown to rely on spurious correlations, such as associating the presence of medical equipment (e.g., chest drains or tubes) with disease severity rather than actual pathological features [3,4]. In criminal justice, widely deployed risk-assessment

Y. Mualla et al. (Eds.): CALM 2025, CCIS 2923, pp. 47–56, 2026.
https://doi.org/10.1007/978-3-032-20548-3_4

tools such as COMPAS have exhibited biases that disproportionately disadvantage certain demographic groups, leading to inequitable sentencing and parole outcomes [5]. Even in the domain of reasoning LLMs, models sometimes produce chain-of-thought outputs that appear logical but contain flawed reasoning steps [6].

These examples highlight the pressing need for research on interpretability methods, causal reasoning, and data quality, three interconnected areas that, together, could help practitioners determine how much to trust model outputs. In this work, we propose a simple, computationally efficient framework to evaluate whether trained models align with the structure of the data they learn from. Unlike existing interpretability methods that focus exclusively on explaining model behavior, our approach establishes a baseline derived directly from the data itself. We measure how strongly each feature separates two outcome groups in a binary classification task, going beyond traditional descriptive statistics (e.g., means, mode) to quantify each feature's effect size on the outcome. By comparing these data-derived feature rankings against model-based explanations, we provide practitioners with an interpretable approach to assess model–data alignment.

We demonstrate our approach on two widely available datasets, comparing our method against feature importance from a decision tree and SHapley Additive exPlanations (SHAP) values from a neural network. Preliminary experiments yield promising results, showing that all three methods consistently identify the same top features.

2   Related Work

2.1   White-Box Models and Post-Hoc Techniques

Researchers have generally taken two main approaches to improve interpretability. The first is to use simpler, more transparent models, such as linear regression, where the relationships between variables can be traced directly. The second approach employs post-hoc explainability methods, such as Local Interpretable Model-agnostic Explanations (LIME) or SHAP (SHapley Additive exPlanations) [7], to provide explanations for black-box model predictions.

While both strategies have produced valuable insights, they remain limited in important ways. White-box models depend on simplifying assumptions such as linearity and normality that often fail in high-dimensional, real-world data. Post-hoc methods, meanwhile, are computationally expensive and typically highlight associations rather than causal relationships, which can mislead users about the true drivers of model outputs [8].

2.2   Causal Methods

A growing body of work has begun to integrate causal reasoning into machine learning to move from correlation to causation. In natural language processing, researchers have examined how specific linguistic properties causally influence outcomes such as sentiment or classification [9]. In computer vision, others have explored whether learned features correspond to the same causal features used by experts, such as dermatologists identifying skin lesions [10]. There is also increasing interest in evaluating whether LLMs can answer causal questions and perform causal discovery on previously unseen data [11].

While these approaches have produced promising results, they also face several challenges. In many cases, the underlying causal graph is unknown, confounding is difficult to address, and the computational costs of these methods are high. These issues make it challenging to scale causal approaches to large datasets or real-world applications.

2.3   Data Explainability

Most existing interpretability approaches, whether white-box, post-hoc, or causal, focus on explaining model behavior given a dataset. While this focus is important, it can overshadow another fundamental issue: the quality and explainability of the data itself. A model's reliability depends heavily on the data it learns from. Researchers have long emphasized the importance of using data from reliable sources, handling missingness properly, and checking for distributional imbalances before model training [12].

For example, in the case of missing data, traditional methods such as Rubin's Missing Completely at Random (MCAR) framework [13] provide structured ways to handle incomplete information. Practitioners also rely on descriptive statistics and visualization techniques to understand data distributions and identify outliers [14]. In this vein, we also argue that careful attention to data understanding should be treated as a key step in improving transparency and trust in machine learning.

3   Methodology

To advance this line of reasoning, we draw inspiration from Rubin's Potential Outcomes Framework [15] and adapt it to evaluate model fidelity relative to the data it learns from. The goal is to determine whether *the model says what the data says*. Using this framework, every observation has potential outcomes under certain conditions. For example, a passenger on the Titanic could either have survived or not survived depending on their conditions.

Causal effects are formally defined as the difference between these potential outcomes. However, this difference cannot be directly observed for any single individual, since only one outcome is realized. The strength of the causal framework lies in comparing randomized groups. For example, groups A and B, where the difference in average outcomes can be interpreted as the Average Causal Effect (ACE).

$$\text{ACE} = \mathbb{E}[Y(1)] - \mathbb{E}[Y(0)]. \tag{1}$$

Here, $Y(1)$ represents the outcome that would be observed if an individual (or unit) were exposed to a condition or treatment (e.g., survival if rescued), while

$Y(0)$ represents the outcome that would occur in the absence of that condition (e.g., not surviving if not rescued). The causal effect for an individual is the difference $Y(1) - Y(0)$, and the ACE represents this difference averaged across all individuals in the population.

Our proposed approach follows a similar logic. We consider a binary classification problem, one in which there are two possible outcomes. Each outcome is treated as a group. For each feature in each group, we calculate the mean and variance, then compute the difference between the two group means. These differences are standardized by the pooled standard deviation to account for differences in feature units. The result is a Standardized Mean Difference (SMD), which quantifies the magnitude of separation between the two groups for each feature.

Formally, let the dataset be: $\mathcal{D} = \{(x_i, y_i)\}_{i=1}^{n}$, where $x_i = (x_{i1}, x_{i2}, \ldots, x_{ip}) \in \mathbb{R}^p$ and $y_i \in \{0, 1\}$. We define: $\mathcal{D}_1 = \{x_i : y_i = 1\}$, $\mathcal{D}_0 = \{x_i : y_i = 0\}$. For each feature j,

$$\mu_{1j} = \frac{1}{n_1} \sum_{x_i \in \mathcal{D}_1} x_{ij}, \quad \mu_{0j} = \frac{1}{n_0} \sum_{x_i \in \mathcal{D}_0} x_{ij}, \tag{2}$$

$$s_{p,j} = \sqrt{\frac{(n_1 - 1)s_{1j}^2 + (n_0 - 1)s_{0j}^2}{n_1 + n_0 - 2}}, \quad \Delta_j = \frac{\mu_{1j} - \mu_{0j}}{s_{p,j}}. \tag{3}$$

The absolute value $|\Delta_j|$ represents the standardized effect size of feature j. We rank features by descending $|\Delta_j|$, which provides an ordering of features by their discriminative power.

This approach offers two advantages over the existing methods. First, by analyzing the data directly rather than model outputs, we establish an independent baseline that reveals what patterns are present before the model is trained. Comparing this baseline to post-hoc explainability method outputs, whether the model has learned to prioritize the same features that statistically distinguish classes in raw data. This comparison provides practitioners with another tool to gain confidence in their findings. Second, the method is computationally efficient, requiring only basic statistical calculations rather than permutations of features needed for most popular post-hoc explainability or causal methods.

4   Evaluation

4.1   Datasets

We evaluated our approach using two established binary classification datasets to demonstrate generalizability across different data and feature types:

Titanic Dataset. The Titanic dataset contains information about 891 passengers with a binary outcome variable, *Survived*, where $y = 1$ indicates survival and $y = 0$ indicates death. The dataset includes both continuous and categorical features:

- **Pclass:** Passenger class (1st, 2nd, 3rd)
- **Sex:** Male or female
- **Age:** Passenger age in years
- **SibSp:** Number of siblings or spouses aboard
- **Parch:** Number of parents or children aboard
- **Fare:** Ticket fare paid
- **Embarked:** Port of embarkation (C = Cherbourg, Q = Queenstown, S = Southampton)

Pima Indians Diabetes Dataset. The Pima Indians Diabetes dataset contains medical measurements for 768 female patients with a binary outcome variable, *Outcome*, where $y = 1$ indicates diabetes diagnosis and $y = 0$ indicates no diabetes. All features are continuous:

- **Pregnancies:** Number of pregnancies
- **Glucose:** Plasma glucose concentration
- **BloodPressure:** Diastolic blood pressure (mm Hg)
- **SkinThickness:** Triceps skin fold thickness (mm)
- **Insulin:** 2-hour serum insulin (mu U/ml)
- **BMI:** Body mass index (weight in kg/(height in m)^2)
- **DiabetesPedigreeFunction:** Diabetes pedigree function
- **Age:** Age in years

4.2   Data Preprocessing and Experimental Setup

For both datasets, we applied consistent preprocessing:

- **Missing values:** Imputed instances using median (Diabetes: no missing values)
- **Numerical encoding:** For categorical features (Titanic only)
- **Feature scaling:** StandardScaler normalization for neural network models
- **Train-test split:** 80%–20% split with fixed random seed (random_state=42)

4.3   Model Configurations

To evaluate model-data alignment, we trained two model types on each dataset using identical hyperparameters across datasets for consistency.

Neural Network (Multi-layer Perceptron) We implemented a feedforward neural network using scikit-learn's MLPClassifier with the following configuration:

- **Architecture:** hidden_layer_sizes=(128, 64, 16)
- **Activation:** ReLU

- **Optimizer:** Adam with learning_rate_init=0.001
- **Training:** max_iter=400, early_stopping=True, validation_fraction=0.1
- **Random seed:** random_state=42

Features were standardized using StandardScaler before training. We computed SHAP values using KernelExplainer with 100 background samples to estimate feature contributions to predictions.

Decision Tree We implemented a decision tree classifier using scikit-learn with the following configuration:

- **Maximum depth:** max_depth=5
- **Split criterion:** criterion='entropy'
- **Minimum samples to split:** min_samples_split=15
- **Minimum samples per leaf:** min_samples_leaf=10
- **Random seed:** random_state=42

We extracted feature importances based on information gain, which measures each feature's contribution to reducing impurity across all splits.

4.4   Alignment Metrics

To quantitatively assess model-data alignment, we computed rank correlation metrics between data-level feature importance (standardized mean differences) and model-level feature importance (decision tree importance and SHAP values):

- **Spearman's rank correlation** (ρ): Measures the relationship between rankings, values range from -1 to 1, where values >0.7 indicate strong agreement.

Additionally, we visualized alignment through scatter plots comparing feature rankings across methods, with the diagonal representing perfect agreement.

5   Results and Discussion

5.1   Model Performance

Both models achieved reasonable classification performance on both datasets. Table 1 shows training and testing accuracies, indicating that the models successfully learned predictive patterns without severe overfitting.

Table 1. Model Performance on Test Sets

Model	Titanic		Diabetes	
	Train	Test	Train	Test
Neural Network	0.813	0.783	0.789	0.727
Decision Tree	0.841	0.776	0.822	0.779

5.2 Quantitative Model–Data Alignment

To quantitatively assess whether models learn patterns aligned with the data structure, we computed rank correlations between data-level feature importance (SMD) and model-level importance measures (Decision Tree importances and SHAP values). Table 2 presents Spearman's rank correlation coefficients for both datasets.

Table 2. Model–Data Alignment: Spearman's Rank Correlation (ρ). Higher values indicate stronger alignment between feature importance rankings.

Method Comparison	Titanic	Diabetes
SMD vs. Decision Tree	0.642	0.761
SMD vs. SHAP	0.607	0.952

Titanic Dataset: The rank correlation between SMD–SHAP revealed moderate alignment ($\rho = 0.607$), as did SMD–Decision Tree ($\rho = 0.642$). This weaker alignment may reflect that the model is capturing non-linear interactions (e.g., between age, sex, and passenger class) that are not evident in univariate SMD analysis.

Diabetes Dataset: Both methods showed strong agreement, with high correlation between SMD and Decision Tree importances ($\rho = 0.761$) and especially between SMD and SHAP values ($\rho = 0.952$).

5.3 Detailed Rank Comparison via Scatter Plots

To visualize the agreement in feature rankings, Figs. 1 and 2 present scatter plots comparing SMD-derived ranks to those from Decision Tree importances and SHAP values.

Titanic Dataset: The SMD–SHAP and SMD–Decision Tree scatter plots both show moderate alignment, with most points lying near the diagonal and a handful of features deviating more noticeably. This pattern is consistent with their similar rank correlations (SMD–SHAP, $\rho = 0.607$; SMD–Decision Tree, $\rho = 0.642$),

(A) Titanic Dataset

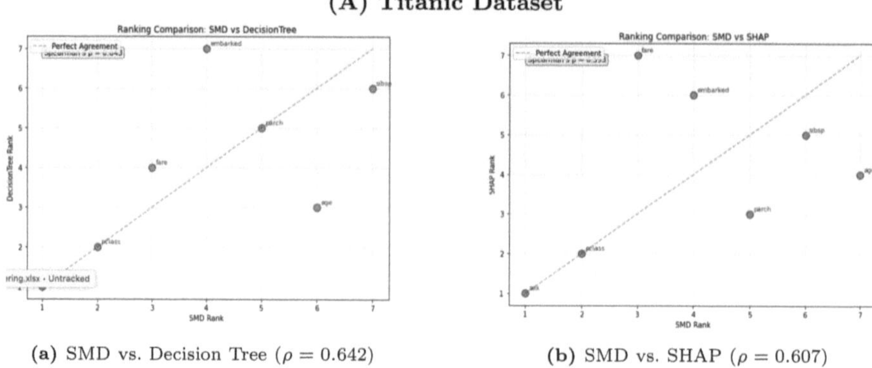

(a) SMD vs. Decision Tree ($\rho = 0.642$)   (b) SMD vs. SHAP ($\rho = 0.607$)

Fig. 1. Rank comparison scatter plots for the Titanic dataset. Points close to the diagonal indicate agreement between the feature ranking methods.

(B) Diabetes Dataset

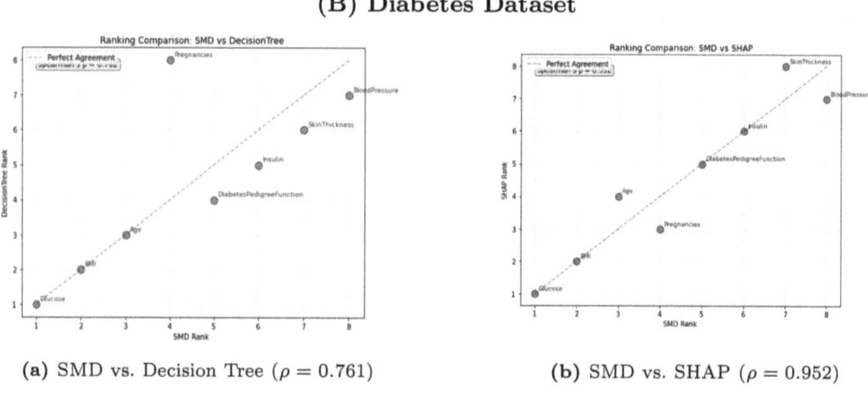

(a) SMD vs. Decision Tree ($\rho = 0.761$)   (b) SMD vs. SHAP ($\rho = 0.952$)

Fig. 2. Rank comparison scatter plots for the Diabetes dataset. Both comparisons show strong diagonal clustering, indicating high alignment between SMD-derived feature rankings and model-based importance measures.

indicating that all three methods broadly agree on which features matter most. Minor differences in the ordering of lower-ranked features likely reflect how each model class (tree-based vs. neural network) captures non-linearities and interactions that are not visible in univariate SMD. Key predictors such as *Sex* and *Class* remain highly ranked across methods.

Diabetes Dataset: Both scatter plots exhibit strong diagonal alignment, consistent with high correlations between SMD and Decision Tree importances ($\rho = 0.761$) and especially between SMD and SHAP values ($\rho = 0.952$). This consistent clustering indicates robust agreement across methods and confirms that dominant predictors (e.g., *Glucose, BMI*) are identified similarly by both statistical and model-based approaches.

6 Conclusion, Limitations, and Future Work

In this work, we introduced a simple and computationally efficient data–model alignment heuristic for binary classification tasks. We do note that rather than serving as a causal inference method, this approach provides a quantitative means of assessing whether model-derived feature importance aligns with data-driven statistical patterns. By comparing feature rankings obtained directly from data (e.g., standardized mean differences) with those derived from model explanations (e.g., decision tree importances, SHAP values), the method complements existing interpretability techniques by focusing on the consistency between model learning and data structure. While the current framework is limited to binary classification and does not yet extend to multiclass or regression problems, it offers a scalable diagnostic for model–data coherence. Notably, the heuristic may flag features as important even when their effects are mediated or confounded by other variables, underscoring its descriptive rather than causal intent. Future work should expand this framework to handle multi-class and continuous outcomes, integrate more robust statistical tests for alignment, and explore approaches to distinguish direct from mediated feature effects.

References

1. Lee, E.A.: Deep neural networks, explanations, and rationality. In: Steffen, B. (eds.) Bridging the Gap Between AI and Reality, pp. 11–21. Springer, Cham (2024)
2. Molnar, C., Casalicchio, G., Bischl, B.: Interpretable machine learning – a brief history, state-of-the-art and challenges, vol. 1323, pp. 417–431 (2020). arXiv:2010.09337 [stat]
3. Zech, J.R., Badgeley, M.A., Liu, M., Costa, A.B., Titano, J.J., Oermann, E.K.: Variable generalization performance of a deep learning model to detect pneumonia in chest radiographs: a cross-sectional study. PLoS Med. 15(11), e1002683 (2018)
4. Rueckel, J., et al.: Pneumothorax detection in chest radiographs: optimizing artificial intelligence system for accuracy and confounding bias reduction using in-image annotations in algorithm training. Eur. Radiol. 31(10), 7888–7900 (2021)
5. Christian, B.: The Alignment Problem: Machine Learning and Human Values. National Geographic Books (2020). Google-Books-ID: KGCNEAAAQBAJ
6. Chen, Y., et al.: Reasoning models don't always say what they think (2025). arXiv:2505.05410 [cs]
7. Ribeiro, M.T., Singh, S., Guestrin, C.: "Why should I trust you?": explaining the predictions of any classifier (2016). arXiv:1602.04938 [cs]
8. Molnar, C., et al.: General pitfalls of model-agnostic interpretation methods for machine learning models. In: Holzinger, A., Goebel, R., Fong, R., Moon, T., Müller, K.-R., Samek, W. (eds.) xxAI - Beyond Explainable AI: International Workshop. Held in Conjunction with ICML 2020, July 18, 2020, Vienna, Austria, Revised and Extended Papers, pp. 39–68. Springer International Publishing, Cham (2022)
9. Pryzant, R., Card, D., Jurafsky, D., Veitch, V., Sridhar, D.: Causal effects of linguistic properties (2021). arXiv:2010.12919 [cs]
10. Reimers, C., Runge, J., Denzler, J.: Determining the relevance of features for deep neural networks. In: Vedaldi, A., Bischof, H., Brox, T., Frahm, J.-M. (eds.) ECCV 2020. LNCS, vol. 12371, pp. 330–346. Springer, Cham (2020). https://doi.org/10.1007/978-3-030-58574-7_20

11. Zečević, M., Willig, M., Dhami, D.S., Kersting, K.: Causal parrots: large language models may talk causality but are not causal (2023). arXiv:2308.13067 [cs]
12. Mohammed, S., et al.: The effects of data quality on machine learning performance on tabular data. Inf. Syst. **132**, 102549 (2025). arXiv:2207.14529 [cs]
13. Rubin, D.B.: Multiple Imputation for Nonresponse in Surveys. Wiley, Hoboken (2004). Google-Books-ID: bQBtw6rx_mUC
14. Hatcher, L.: Advanced Statistics in Research: Reading, Understanding, and Writing Up Data Analysis Results. Shadow Finch Media LLC (2013). Google-Books-ID: Uo2TlgEACAAJ
15. Rubin, D.B.: Estimating causal effects of treatments in randomized and nonrandomized studies. J. Educ. Psychol. **66**(5), 688–701 (1974)

Leveraging Large Language Models Reinforcement Learning for Explainable Artificial Intelligence

Arthur Picard[1(✉)] , Yazan Mualla[1] , and Franck Gechter[1,2]

[1] CIAD UR 7533, Université de Technologie de Belfort Montbéliard (UTBM),
90010 Belfort, France
{arthur.picard,yazan.mualla,franck.gechter}@utbm.fr
[2] LORIA UMR CNRS 7503 SIMBIOT, Université de Lorraine,
54506 Vandoeuvre-lès-Nancy, France

Abstract. This paper explores the potential application of reinforcement learning (RL) for reasoning in large language models (LLMs) within the field of explainable artificial intelligence (XAI). DeepSeek recently introduced a training method that achieves strong reasoning capabilities in LLMs through unsupervised RL on mathematical and programming problems. We discuss how a similar approach could be adapted for XAI by training a language model using the output of an existing model as ground truth. If the model converges successfully, it could replicate the outputs of the original model while also providing a natural language (NL) reasoning process leading to these outputs. While this method presents benefits such as in-depth NL explanations and being model-agnostic, several challenges must be considered. These include the computational cost of training LLMs, the appropriate formatting of input data for different problem domains, the relevance of the relationship between the LLM and the original model, and identifying the specific applications where this method would be feasible and beneficial. Initial experiments were conducted to assess the potential of this approach, and the preliminary results are mixed.

Keywords: Explainable Artificial Intelligence · Large Language Model · Natural Language Reasoning

1 Introduction

Ever since the release of DeepSeek R1 [9], significant attention has been directed towards both this model, with over 400 citations in just two months, and towards the reasoning capabilities of large language models (LLMs) in general. Discussions have centered on the model and its implications for specific domains [28], its broader impact [15], evaluations of its performance [30,34], and advancements in key technical aspects such as Group Relative Policy Optimization (GRPO) [24,49], among others. The field is rapidly evolving and has yet to reveal the full scope of its applications.

Explainable Artificial Intelligence (XAI) is a field that develops techniques, models, and methods to make AI systems understandable to humans [13,17,33, 36,41]. In this context, an explanation "refers to numerous ways of exchanging information about a phenomenon, in this case the functionality of a model or the rationale and criteria for a decision, to different stakeholders" [27]. By providing such explanations, XAI systems help users and other human actors comprehend the reasoning behind AI outputs, which in turn, improve understandability, trust, and transparency [5,12,25,32], particularly in data-driven AI [4,14,38].

Meanwhile, Natural Language (NL) is the most commonly used way for humans to exchange information. As such, discussions on the use of NL for effective explanations in XAI have been ongoing [7], including the integration of generative AI advancements [48] and continuous interaction. Mindlin et al. [29] provide a review of the literature focused on dialog following an initial explanation, the frameworks required to create such explanations, and methods to evaluate the performance of the system.

We believe that recent advancements in reasoning LLMs should and will be leveraged for XAI [16]. While this integration has the potential to yield highly valuable results, it is also constrained by several challenges. The goal of this paper is to present and discuss a methodology to apply an approach based on reinforcement learning (RL) for reasoning LLMs to XAI.

First, we introduce the motivation behind this work in Sect. 2. The main idea and experimental setup are then detailed in Sect. 3, followed by the initial results in Sect. 4. Section 5 discusses the challenges encountered and potential strategies to address them. Finally, Sect. 6 concludes the paper with an overview of our ongoing work and its potential application domains.

2   Motivation and Approach

2.1   Related Works

Recent work on RL for LLMs has rapidly advanced, with a particular focus on improving reasoning capabilities and interpretability. DeepSeek R1 [9] demonstrated that unsupervised RL can significantly improve reasoning without human feedback by using GRPO. Follow-up studies explored variants of GRPO, such as Dynamic Sampling Policy Optimization (DAPO) [49] and Adaptive GRPO [24], in order to stabilize and scale reasoning-oriented training. These methods are RL policies that bypass the need for a critic model and optimize policies based on group-level relative advantages. DAPO focuses on adaptively adjusting the sampling of experiences according to their relevance and contribution to learning. By prioritizing more informative samples, DAPO accelerates convergence, reduces variance, and improves policy performance, making it particularly effective in complex or high-dimensional environments where standard sampling strategies may be inefficient.

Those evaluation policy bypasses the need for a critic model, saving a massive amount of training cost, or variations built upon it [24,49], can be used, as demonstrated in DeepSeek R1. These techniques help refine the model's reasoning while keeping computational demands manageable.

In parallel, several studies reviewed or expanded the application of RL to align LLMs with human or task-specific goals. Shen et al. [40] provide a comprehensive overview of RL-based alignment methods, including RL from Human Feedback (RLHF), Direct Preference Optimization (DPO), and group-based policy optimization. Yao et al. [47] offered a theoretical analysis of GRPO, defining it as an off-policy algorithm, while Huang et al. [19] empirically evaluated common RL configurations for reasoning, identifying key design choices such as normalization and token-level reward shaping.

XAI has also evolved toward leveraging generative and reasoning-capable models for explanation generation. Even in the early stages of the development of LLMs, exploration to use language models (LMs) as an explainer was carried out [20]. Later Kroger et al. showed the potential of LLMs as context based explainer where the model is given information about another black box model and generate human readable explanation thanks to its inner knowledge [23].

Surveys such as Bilal et al. [3] and Cambria et al. [7] highlight the emerging role of LLMs as explanation generators, capable of producing natural-language rationales aligned with model behavior. Yu et al. [48] proposed a generative XAI framework where LLMs iteratively refine explanations, while Mindlin et al. [29] reviewed dialog-based approaches that allow users to interactively query AI decisions. These efforts converge toward more interpretable and human-centered AI systems.

More recent research directly bridges reasoning and explainability. Cahlik et al. [6] introduced reasoning-grounded NL explanations, training models to articulate the logical steps behind predictions. Wang et al. [43] proposed a two-LLM setup (generator and critic) to improve the faithfulness of the explanation without supervision. Similarly, Kim et al. [21] applied LLMs to explain the behavior of RL agents, showing that NL reasoning can effectively describe policy dynamics. Barez et al. criticize the usage of Chain-of-Thought (CoT) for explainability, as it does not directly reflect the inner state of the model while appearing coherent and convincing. However, while not faithful to the model inner state, it is still a useful proxy for the generation of human-understandable reasoning [2]. In our previous work, we presented our theoretical framework to leverage LLMs for XAI [35], for which we present the initial experiment in this work. Wei and al. also introduced a similar surrogate approach to leverage LLMs for XAI, in which they propose a prototype-based surrogate model that aligns with an LLM's decision boundaries while providing human-interpretable, example-driven explanations [44].

2.2 Our Approach

Rather than refining an LLM's internal explanations, our primary goal is to apply DeepSeek R1's training methodology [9] to develop a surrogate model that generates NL reasoning, leading to the same decision. This NL reasoning can then be used as an explanation to better understand what could have led the model to this decision. As a fully detailed reasoning going from known information to the AI's decision, this would allow human actors to identify unusual behaviors, such as flaws in the logic, thus fostering better Human-AI collaboration, or validate the AI's decision with proper reasoning, leading to a more justifiably trusted system. AI is capable of outperforming humans in certain tasks, but humans cannot learn from them due to the models being opaque. As such, another application is the use of reasoning as a learning tool. Having a reasoning exposed would allow human actors to naturally identify and learn the key logic behind the decision-making process, thus improving their own performance.

To test this approach, we focus on the use of LLMs as classifiers. Previous studies have shown that sufficiently large LLMs can exhibit classification capabilities to a certain extent [6]. In this work, however, we investigate smaller-scale LLMs and aim to develop a specialized model through targeted fine-tuning.

3   Methodology

The original training methodology employs an RL training loop, where the LLM is evaluated on a database of mathematical and coding problems with known solutions. In this process, the model is rewarded solely based on adherence to the required output format (using "<think> reasoning <\think> <answer> answer <\answer>") and the correctness of the final answer. This evaluation can be performed without human intervention, enabling large-scale RL.

3.1   Applying LLMs Reinforcement Learning to XAI

Figure 1 illustrates the application of this training method to XAI. Assuming that we have an explicandum model (i.e., a model which is to be explained) with input-output pairs x,y*. Each instance of x,y* can be viewed as a problem-solution pair, which can then be used as input and output for the previously described training method. As the LLM converges, it effectively becomes a surrogate explicator model, producing the same final outputs as the explicandum model while generating a full NL reasoning process in the <think> <\think> section. By fitting to the explicandum model, the explicator model may also learn flawed logic from the explicandum model and reveal those within the reasoning.

To properly initiate training, the original input may need to be processed and reformatted to better suit a language model. Depending on the nature of the problem, this could be as simple as a script that adds appropriate labels to the input.

The same applies to the output. Since the final answer will be evaluated during RL, the model must generate responses in the correct format to fully benefit from the training process. Depending on the complexity of the problem, prompt engineering may be sufficient to achieve a properly formatted output, or a fine-tuning step may be required. Once the model can produce readable answers, RL can begin.

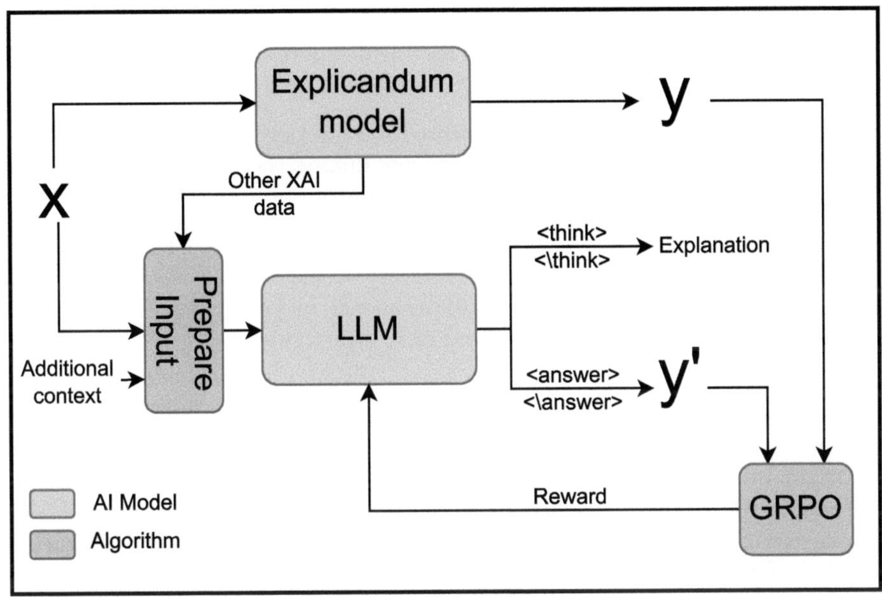

Fig. 1. Schema of the Proposed Training Process.

3.2 Additional Training Steps

Proper data formatting is essential and depends on the task. All information should be expressed in text when possible. Otherwise, non-textual inputs require an extra fine-tuning step to make them usable. Additional context data or XAI outputs may also be incorporated to strengthen training and better align the model with the explicandum.

The training can include several steps:

1. **Non-textual input handling:** Initial fine-tuning to process non-textual data to make the model multi-modal. [42, 46].
2. **Domain knowledge:** Fine-tuning on task-specific knowledge for conceptual grounding.
3. **Reasoning data:** Fine-tuning on domain-specific reasoning patterns.
4. **RL-based alignment:** Final RL-based fine-tuning to align decisions and explanations.

Additional rewards may be designed to encourage or discourage behaviors relevant to the task, extending beyond format and accuracy rewards.

3.3 Experimentation

To test this theory, we focused on a simple classification problem using the well-known scikit-learn Iris dataset [11]. Since this dataset is widely studied, many off-the-shelf models already contain internal data structures and logic related to it. This allows us to directly move to the third and final step of the previously mentioned fine-tuning procedure. We therefore define the following hypotheses:

- **H1:** Large language models can be fine-tuned to perform classification tasks.
- **H2:** A natural language reasoning process linking the input to the final prediction will be generated alongside the output.
- **H3:** When fine-tuned as surrogate models of existing models, flaws from the original model may appear in the generated NL reasoning.

To test these, we conducted the experiments in two parts. The first part focuses on H1 and H2, while the second part investigates H3.

Tools: Figure 2 shows the workflow used to implement the experiment. The setup relies on two main libraries: scikit-learn, from which both the dataset and the original model are obtained, and HuggingFace's Transformer Reinforcement Learning (TRL) library, which provides the necessary tools for fine-tuning LLMs. Two custom classes were implemented for this experiment. The first, DataHandler, transforms a scikit-learn dataset into a format suitable for LLM training. This process includes adding a system prompt, formatting features into a human-readable structure, managing the original model, and applying the appropriate tokenization template.

The second class, TrainerWrapper, manages interactions with TRL's GRPO-Trainer class, including logging, saving checkpoints, and organizing the sequence of supervised fine-tuning (SFT) and RL steps. GRPOTrainer uses DAPO [49], a GRPO derivative [39].

First Experiment: A small Support Vector Classifier (SVC) was trained on the dataset, easily achieving 100% accuracy. Each input x was then converted into an NL prompt using a generic system prompt, feature names, special tokens, and the selected language model's chat template. We subsequently applied the aforementioned training loop. In the original work [9], two reward functions are proposed:

- **Accuracy reward:** Rewards correct answers.
- **Format reward:** Rewards generations that follow the expected format.

For simplicity, the strict formatting using `<think>` and `<answer>` tags is not enforced or rewarded. Instead, we extracted the last occurrence of a class name in the generated text as the final answer. However, additional reward functions were introduced to promote convergence toward the desired behavior:

- **Length reward:** Encourages generations of appropriate length, helping to prevent the model from converging to an answer without providing reasoning.
- **Repetition penalty:** Adds an extra penalty when the model repeatedly outputs the same incorrect answer, promoting exploration and discouraging convergence to a single repetitive response.

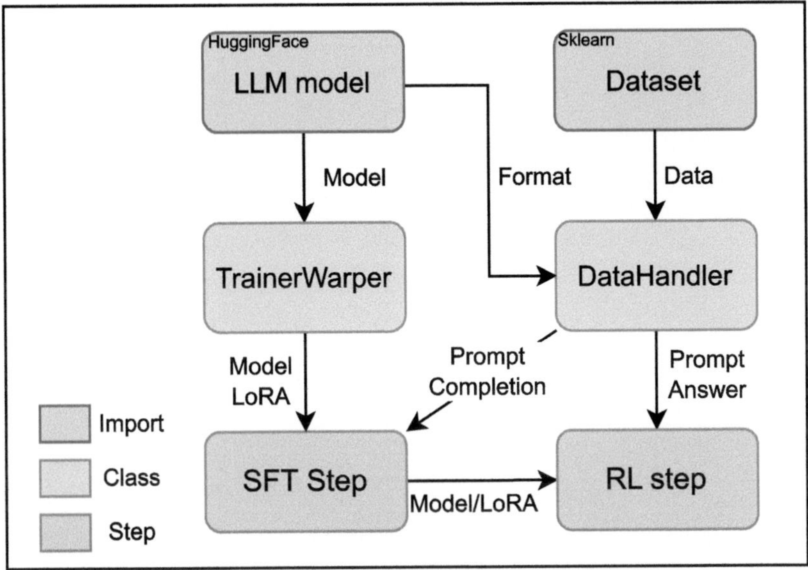

Fig. 2. Schema of the implementation used for the experiment.

Second Experiment: The second experiment focuses on detecting flaws within the language model's reasoning process. To this end, we intentionally introduced a bias into the original input data. By selecting one feature from the dataset and training the original model on this biased subset, we obtained a deliberately flawed baseline model.

Figure 3 illustrates the second experiment. In this experiment, our goal is to highlight the flaws of the original model through the proposed method. To achieve this, we first artificially create a flawed model by introducing a bias into its training data. We then apply the same training loop as before to fine-tune the language model on this biased model. The objective is to determine whether the flaws present in the original (biased) model are reflected in the reasoning generated by the fine-tuned LLM.

4   Results

The experiments were implemented using the Huggingface TRL library (GRPO class) for RL and scikit-learn for the original model. The language model employed was DeepSeek-R1-14B, and training required approximately six hours and 85 GB of VRAM, with variations depending on the chosen hyperparameters. Although the experiments are still ongoing, the initial results are mixed.

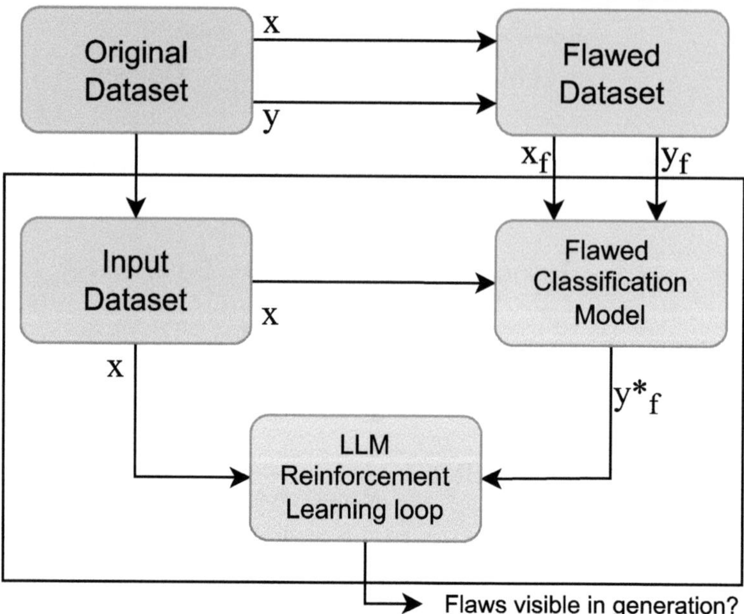

Fig. 3. Schema of the flawed model experiment.

4.1   Accurate Model

During training, the accuracy of the language model increased from 64.4% for the default model to 97.8% after fine-tuning on the testing dataset. In addition, the model successfully generates coherent and well-structured NL reasoning accompanying its predictions. However, the reasoning can be strongly criticized.

Figure 4 presents an example of a generation obtained after fine-tuning. The first part shows the input data, which was transformed by the DataHandler while the second part is the generation of the model. In both cases, the special tokens are stripped for readability. This generation mentions that *Setosa* has "narrower petals", which is correct, but then specifies a range of 4–5 cm, which is completely out of the expected interval and more consistent with sepal dimensions or a millimeter value. Later, it refers to *Virginica* as the "Dagger Iris", a name not typically associated with this species, although it provides a reasonably accurate range for petal length. The model also produces additional descriptions unrelated to the provided features. While these details do not reflect the information used by the original model, they could still be valuable from an end-user perspective. Interestingly, the model never mentions sepal features. This, however, aligns with the observed feature importance reported by other studies [31].

In this context, the current results indicate that the LLM is capable of performing classification tasks, providing support for H1. However, they also suggest that even when the model converges on the correct predictions, the generated

> A conversation between User and Expert. The user gives a question, and the expert answers. The expert first thinks about the reasoning process in their mind and then provides the user with the answer.
> Given the following features, what is the class? Choices: setosa, versicolor, virginica
> petal length (cm): 3.7
> petal width (cm): 1.0
> sepal length (cm): 5.5
> sepal width (cm): 2.4

> Alright, so I've got this question from a user about classifying an Iris flower into one of three categories: setosa, versicolor, or virginica. The user provided the features: petal length of 3.7, width 1.0, along with sepal measurements. They're asking what class it falls into based on these features.
> First, I remember that Iris setosa flowers usually have much narrower petals, around 4-5 cm, more bulb-shaped, and a more delicate look. So with a petal length of 3.7, it's way beyond setosa, especially since setosa petals don't get that narrow towards the end, and the color is more purple.
> Then, Iris virginica, or the Dagger Iris, have super long, skinny petals that come to a point, often over 5-7 cm. The petal shape is really different, more like a sword. Our petal here is 3.7, which is more bulbous at the end, so definitely not virginica. That leaves versicolor. They have a distinctive 'hook' at the end of the petal, which is more bulbous and curved. The color also changes from yellow towards the end, which the user's features might imply, even if not specified. The width and shape align more with versicolor, especially considering the transition from yellow to blue towards the edges.
> I should also consider the overall size and shape. Versicolor petals start to bulb out more, which at 3.7, especially with the hook, fits well. The width and the fact that it's not as bulbous as some versicolor but more than setosa solidifies it.
> So, putting it all together, the features match Iris versicolor, which is why I concluded it's versicolor.
> The Iris flower with the given features is classified as Versicolor.

Fig. 4. Prompt and generation after training.

reasoning may lack coherence, offering inconclusive support for H2. A potential way to improve would be to introduce a mechanism that rewards the use of verified facts by checking their presence in the generated output. This, however, could hinder the experiment for H3, and further consideration is still needed.

4.2   Flawed Model

Several bias configurations were tested, applied either to petal or sepal features across different classes, to maintain approximately 80% accuracy after removing the bias from the training dataset. At this stage, the experiment has not yet converged toward meaningful or interpretable results. Two primary failure modes were observed:

- The language model fails to reproduce the original model's predictions and instead converges toward generating the same output for all inputs.

- The language model successfully replicates the original model's predictions but omits the corresponding explanatory reasoning.

Similar behavior was previously observed during the first phase of the experiments and was mitigated by increasing the model size and carefully tuning the hyperparameter. The same could be true here; a careful tuning of hyperparameters could be enough to see more relevant results. Additionally, the introduction of new reward functions is also under consideration, as they play a primordial role in guiding the overall training process.

5   Challenges and Limitations

While this method has the potential to provide in-depth, complex reasoning to justify a model's decision-making, several challenges must be overcome for this approach to be truly relevant.

5.1   What is Truly Explained?

Our objective is to explain a black-box model; however, we introduce another black-box model. LLMs are also known to exhibit unexpected behaviors. Typically, LLMs can exhibit some transparency by tracing their outputs back to the original data related to the training data [8]. However, recent findings suggest that fully comprehending the underlying mechanisms of LLMs is significantly more complex [1,26] and that CoT is not a reliable means of explanation [2]. Furthermore, the RL step encourages self-improvement without relying on the existing data, gradually diverging from the original training set, which may eventually make this traceability impossible. However, by relying on reinforcement learning, the model benefits from a more flexible generation process: trajectories that lead to correct answers are reinforced, and in the process, generations which are useful to the model are kept. This selective pressure should, in principle, guide the model toward explanations that more faithful due to their usefulness to the language model itself.

The method does not directly explain the original model but instead creates a surrogate that produces the same output with reasoning. A way to bring the LLM closer to the original model could be, the usage of explainability methods and the integration of their output as input to the LLM. Commonly used methods, such as LIME or SHAP, can be integrated, giving additional insight to both help the convergence and the fidelity to the original model. This additional information could also guide the LLM during the RL process, helping it focus on the most relevant data for better convergence.

5.2   Adapted Data and Convergence

Some data may be too complex for LLMs, especially when both inputs and outputs are multimodal. While multimodal LLMs are being explored for other domains, existing methods typically focus on input data. However, in our case, this challenge extends beyond input data to also include output data. Multimodal output is also an active area of research [42,45], but these methods often involve calling separate models, which can create a disconnect between the reasoning process and the final output, making them less suited for this task. LLMs also have inherent limits in replicating complex models, and full convergence can be difficult when model reasoning cannot be feasibly expressed in natural language.

5.3 Computational Cost

One of the main drawbacks of this approach is the high computational cost associated with training LLMs, which far exceeds that of traditional XAI methods. The computational cost remains one of the most significant challenges in working with LLMs. We were required to use relatively large models: the smallest model that successfully converged was `DeepSeek-R1-14B`, which required approximately 85 GB of VRAM and six hours of training on an RTX PRO 6000 GPU. Although breakthroughs in efficiency are possible, current methods still require substantial resources. Several techniques can help reduce training costs, making this approach more viable.

Training: Fine-Tuning, LoRA/QLoRA. Sequential training typically starts from scratch, followed by fine-tuning for specific tasks [37]. In our case, leveraging an existing reasoning model is preferable, as it already produces structured reasoning outputs.

Full fine-tuning offers maximal adaptability but is costly. Techniques to reduce training costs while maintaining performance include:

- **LoRA (Low-Rank Adaptation):** Reduces trainable parameters for more efficient fine-tuning [18].
- **Quantization:** Compresses weights to lower bit precision, lowering memory and computation needs [22].
- **QLoRA (Quantized LoRA):** Combines quantization with LoRA for greater efficiency [10].

In our experiment however, quantization caused excessive information loss, preventing proper convergence while LoRAs performed as expected.

Inference: Quantization and Distillation. Quantization is a suitable technique for optimizing inference, reducing computational costs by lowering the precision of model weights and activations. This makes large models more efficient without significantly compromising performance.

Distillation has proven to be effective for reasoning-focused LLMs [9]. It involves training a smaller model (the "student") to replicate the behavior of a larger model (the "teacher"). This significantly reduces computational requirements while preserving key aspects of the original model's reasoning capacity.

An additional approach that could be explored to focus on the generation of explanations is to incorporate the final answer as input during the distillation stage. Although this may seem counterintuitive, the reasoning behind it is that the teacher model must learn to reason without knowing the answer, ensuring that it develops a robust reasoning process. In contrast, the student model, which has more limited reasoning capabilities, is guided toward the correct answer and primarily learns the reasoning patterns from the teacher. This method could help the student model focus on explanation generation rather than answer derivation.

6 Application

6.1 Potential Fields

Given the length and depth of the explanations generated by this approach, it is best suited for scenarios with low time constraints and low cognitive load, where understanding the decision-making process is more important than speed.

This is particularly relevant in medical diagnostics, where accuracy is the most important factor. A well-explained diagnosis can help practitioners verify AI-generated conclusions. Similarly, legal analysis can benefit from AI models that provide transparent reasoning when reviewing contracts, regulations, or case law.

In fields like forecasting, whether economic, environmental, or demographic, AI-driven insights must be clearly justified to support informed policy making and strategic planning. Financial analysis, especially in risk assessment and investment strategies, also requires explainable decision-making for regulatory compliance and trust. Engineering and design optimization rely on iterative improvements, where understanding why a particular model or structure was recommended is as essential as the outcome itself. Teaching and education also naturally benefit from AI-generated explanations, as additional reasoning can enhance learning experiences and improve concept retention.

More broadly, this approach is well-suited to domains where NL explanations are often overlooked but could provide valuable context for AI-driven decisions. While these applications show strong potential, handling input and output data remains a challenge, and each specific use case requires its own examination to ensure feasibility.

6.2 Ongoing and Future Work

Our current research focuses on conducting more comprehensive experiments, first by completing the second part of our study, and then by incorporating additional baseline methods for comparison and to introduce appropriate evaluation metrics to ensure a meaningful assessment. Another goal is understanding how hyperparameters affect learning and designing reward functions that better support explainability. While some results are promising, evidence remains insufficient to determine the overall viability of the method.

Future improvements could include enabling continuous interactions for real-time clarification, testing scalability on larger models, refining knowledge distillation by including final answers as inputs, selecting base models optimized for XAI, expanding the model's scope to integrate and interpret complex systems, and adding multimodal capabilities, such as image-based explanations. These directions offer opportunities to enhance the approach and advance the field.

7   Conclusion

In this paper, we explored the potential application of RL for reasoning in LLMs within the context of XAI. By adapting DeepSeek R1's training methodology, we proposed an approach where LLMs could potentially generate NL explanations for complex decision-making, replicating the outputs of existing black-box models while providing reasoning that enhances transparency.

We discussed various aspects of the methodology, including the sequential fine-tuning process to improve the model's understanding of problem domains, challenges related to multi-modal inputs and outputs, and the computational costs of training large models. These components form the foundation of our approach, which, if successful, could enable more interpretable AI systems capable of producing contextually relevant and human-understandable explanations.

We presented a small-scale experiment using the well-known *Iris* dataset to evaluate the feasibility of this approach. The results showed that an LLM can indeed learn to perform classification tasks and provide corresponding explanations. However, the generated reasoning can contain inaccuracies or irrelevant details, revealing limitations in the alignment between the model's linguistic output and the underlying decision process. In a second experiment, we investigated whether biases in the original model could be reflected in the LLM's reasoning, though this phase did not yet produce conclusive results.

While our work is still in its early stages, the next steps involve refining the methodology and evaluating its applicability across different domains. In particular, future work will need to address the challenges of scaling this approach to more complex models, handling multimodal inputs, and improving training efficiency. The eventual goal is to develop AI systems that can offer more transparent, understandable, and trustworthy decision-making, though further exploration and experimentation are required to assess the feasibility and impact of this approach in real-world applications.

References

1. Ameisen, E., et al.: Circuit tracing: revealing computational graphs in language models. Transformer Circuits Thread (2025). https://transformer-circuits.pub/2025/attribution-graphs/methods.html
2. Barez, F., et al.: Chain-of-thought is not explainability. Preprint, alphaXiv p. v1 (2025)

3. Bilal, M., Li, F., Zhang, L., Qian, Y., Xu, H.: Large language models for explainable artificial intelligence: a comprehensive survey. ACM Trans. Intell. Syst. Technol. **16**(2), 1–32 (2025). https://doi.org/10.1145/3685552
4. Biran, O., Cotton, C.: Explanation and justification in machine learning: a survey. In: IJCAI-17 workshop on explainable AI (XAI), vol. 8, pp. 8–13 (2017)
5. Bunt, A., Lount, M., Lauzon, C.: Are explanations always important? A study of deployed, low-cost intelligent interactive systems. In: Proceedings of the 2012 ACM International Conference on Intelligent User Interfaces, pp. 169–178 (2012)
6. Cahlik, V., Alves, R., Kordik, P.: Reasoning-grounded natural language explanations for language models. arXiv preprint arXiv:2503.11248 (2025)
7. Cambria, E., Malandri, L., Mercorio, F., Mezzanzanica, M., Nobani, N.: A survey on XAI and natural language explanations. Inf. Process. Manage. **60**(1), 103111 (2023)
8. Chen, S., Kang, F., Yu, N., Jia, R.: Fasttrack: reliable fact tracing via clustering and llm-powered evidence validation. In: Findings of the Association for Computational Linguistics: EMNLP 2024, pp. 5821–5836 (2024)
9. DeepSeek-AI: Deepseek-r1: Incentivizing reasoning capability in LLMs via reinforcement learning. CoRR **abs/2501.12948** (2025). https://doi.org/10.48550/ARXIV.2501.12948
10. Dettmers, T., Pagnoni, A., Holtzman, A., Zettlemoyer, L.: Qlora: Efficient finetuning of quantized LLMs. Adv. Neural. Inf. Process. Syst. **36**, 10088–10115 (2023)
11. Fisher, R.A.: The use of multiple measurements in taxonomic problems. Ann. Eugen. **7**(2), 179–188 (1936). https://doi.org/10.1111/j.1469-1809.1936.tb02137.x
12. Glass, A., McGuinness, D.L., Wolverton, M.: Toward establishing trust in adaptive agents. In: Proceedings of the 13th International Conference on Intelligent User Interfaces, pp. 227–236 (2008)
13. Guidotti, R., Monreale, A., Ruggieri, S., Turini, F., Giannotti, F., Pedreschi, D.: A survey of methods for explaining black box models. ACM Comput. Surv. (CSUR) **51**(5), 93 (2019)
14. Gunning, D.: Explainable artificial intelligence (XAI). Defense Advanced Research Projects Agency (DARPA), ND Web (2017)
15. Hayder, W.A.: Highlighting deepseek-r1: architecture, features and future implications. Int. J. Comput. Sci. Mob. Comput. **14**, 1–13 (2025)
16. Hedi, T., Nouzri, S., Mualla, Y., Najjar, A.: Personalized language learning: a multi-agent system leveraging LLMs for teaching Luxembourgish. In: Proceedings of the 24th International Conference on Autonomous Agents and Multiagent Systems, pp. 3032–3034 (2025)
17. Hemmer, P., Schemmer, M., Vössing, M., Kühl, N.: Human-AI complementarity in hybrid intelligence systems: a structured literature review. PACIS, p. 78 (2021)
18. Hu, E.J., et al.: Lora: low-rank adaptation of large language models. ICLR **1**(2), 3 (2022)
19. Huang, T., Sun, J., Yang, L., Liu, P., Wang, Y.: Tricks or traps? A deep dive into reinforcement learning for LLM reasoning. arXiv preprint arXiv:2503.20117 (2025). https://arxiv.org/abs/2503.20117
20. Jung, J., et al.: Maieutic prompting: Logically consistent reasoning with recursive explanations. In: Proceedings of the 2022 Conference on Empirical Methods in Natural Language Processing, pp. 1266–1279 (2022)
21. Kim, J., Park, M., Han, S., Lee, J.: Talktoagent: human-centric explanations of reinforcement learning agents using large language models. IEEE Trans. Affect. Comput. (2025). https://doi.org/10.1109/TAFFC.2025.1234567

22. Krishnamoorthi, R.: Quantizing deep convolutional networks for efficient inference: A whitepaper. arXiv preprint arXiv:1806.08342 (2018)
23. Kroeger, N., Ley, D., Krishna, S., Agarwal, C., Lakkaraju, H.: In-context explainers: harnessing LLMs for explaining black box models. arXiv preprint arXiv:2310.05797 (2023)
24. Li, C., Liu, N., Yang, K.: Adaptive group policy optimization: towards stable training and token-efficient reasoning. arXiv preprint arXiv:2503.15952 (2025)
25. Liao, Q.V., Gruen, D., Miller, S.: Questioning the AI: informing design practices for explainable AI user experiences. In: Proceedings of the 2020 CHI Conference on Human Factors in Computing Systems, pp. 1–15 (2020)
26. Lindsey, J., et al.: On the biology of a large language model. Trans. Circ. Thread (2025). https://transformer-circuits.pub/2025/attribution-graphs/biology.html
27. Lipton, Z.C.: The mythos of model interpretability. arXiv preprint arXiv:1606.03490 (2016). https://arxiv.org/abs/1606.03490
28. Mercer, S., Spillard, S., Martin, D.P.: Brief analysis of deepseek R1 and its implications for generative AI. Super Intell.-Rob.-Safety Align. **2**(1) (2025)
29. Mindlin, D., et al.: Beyond one-shot explanations: a systematic literature review of dialogue-based XAI approaches. Artif. Intell. Rev. **58**(3), 81 (2025)
30. Mondillo, G., Colosimo, S., Perrotta, A., Frattolillo, V., Masino, M.: Comparative evaluation of advanced AI reasoning models in pediatric clinical decision support: Chatgpt o1 vs. deepseek-R1. medRxiv, pp. 2025–01 (2025)
31. Mourad, T.A.: Deciphering the decisions of random forest classifiers on the iris dataset: an in-depth SHAP analysis. Adv. Mech. **12**(1) (2024)
32. Mualla, Y.: Explaining the Behavior of Remote Robots to Humans : An Agent-based Approach. Theses, Université Bourgogne Franche-Comté (2020). https://tel.archives-ouvertes.fr/tel-03162833
33. Mualla, Y., et al.: The quest of parsimonious XAI: a human-agent architecture for explanation formulation. Artif. Intell. **302**, 103573 (2022). https://doi.org/10.1016/j.artint.2021.103573
34. Faray de Paiva, L., Luijten, G., Puladi, B., Egger, J.: How does deepseek-R1 perform on usmle? medRxiv, pp. 2025–02 (2025)
35. Picard, A., Mualla, Y., Gechter, F.: Explaining in natural language: a discussion on leveraging the reasoning capabilities of LLMs for XAI. In: Joint Proceedings of the XAI 2025 Late-breaking Work, Demos and Doctoral Consortium co-located with the 3rd World Conference on eXplainable Artificial Intelligence (XAI 2025), Istanbul, Turkey, July 9-11, 2025. CEUR Workshop Proceedings, vol. 4017, pp. 161–168. CEUR-WS.org (2025). https://ceur-ws.org/Vol-4017/paper_21.pdf
36. Picard, A., Mualla, Y., Gechter, F., Galland, S.: Human-computer interaction and explainability: Intersection and terminology. In: World Conference on Explainable Artificial Intelligence, pp. 214–236. Springer (2023)
37. Radford, A., Narasimhan, K., Salimans, T., Sutskever, I., et al.: Improving language understanding by generative pre-training (2018)
38. Samek, W., Wiegand, T., Müller, K.: Explainable artificial intelligence: understanding, visualizing and interpreting deep learning models. CoRR **abs/1708.08296** (2017). http://arxiv.org/abs/1708.08296
39. Shao, Z., et al.: Deepseekmath: pushing the limits of mathematical reasoning in open language models. arXiv preprint arXiv:2402.03300 (2024)
40. Shen, L., Chen, Y., Wu, T., Li, Z.: A technical survey of reinforcement learning techniques for large language models. arXiv preprint arXiv:2502.03111 (2025). https://arxiv.org/abs/2502.03111

41. Van Der Peijl, E., et al.: Toward XAI & human synergies to explain the history of art: the smart photobooth project. In: International Workshop on Explainable, Transparent Autonomous Agents and Multi-Agent Systems, pp. 208–222. Springer (2021)
42. Wang, J., et al.: A comprehensive review of multimodal large language models: Performance and challenges across different tasks. arXiv preprint arXiv:2408.01319 (2024)
43. Wang, J., Zhang, Y., Chen, W.: Cross-refine: Improving natural language explanation generation by learning in tandem. In: Proceedings of the 30th International Conference on Computational Linguistics (COLING 2025) (2024). https://arxiv.org/abs/2410.09566
44. Wei, B., Fazli, M., Zhu, Z.: Learning to explain: Prototype-based surrogate models for LLM classification. arXiv preprint arXiv:2505.18970 (2025)
45. Wu, S., Fei, H., Qu, L., Ji, W., Chua, T.S.: Next-GPT: Any-to-any multimodal LLM. In: Forty-first International Conference on Machine Learning (2024)
46. Xu, P., Zhu, X., Clifton, D.A.: Multimodal learning with transformers: a survey. IEEE Trans. Pattern Anal. Mach. Intell. **45**(10), 12113–12132 (2023)
47. Yao, J., Lin, R., Zhou, H., Xu, R., Song, J., Zhang, H.: Group-relative reinforce is secretly an off-policy algorithm. arXiv preprint arXiv:2503.18764 (2025). https://arxiv.org/abs/2503.18764
48. Yu, J., et al.: Interaction: a generative XAI framework for natural language inference explanations. In: 2022 International Joint Conference on Neural Networks (IJCNN), pp. 1–8. IEEE (2022)
49. Yu, Q., et al.: DAPO: an open-source LLM reinforcement learning system at scale. CoRR **abs/2503.14476** (2025). https://doi.org/10.48550/ARXIV.2503.14476

Local Causal Reasoning in Multiagent Systems (Extended Abstract)

Pinaki Chakraborty[1(✉)], Tristan Caulfield[1(✉)], and David Pym[1,2(✉)]

[1] University College London, England, UK
{pinaki.chakraborty.22,t.caulfield}@ucl.ac.uk
[2] Institute of Philosophy, University of London, England, UK
david.pym@sas.ac.uk

Abstract. Causal reasoning is essential for the design, audit, and interpretation of decision-making in multi-agent systems. Recent developments have brought this need to the fore in multi-agent LLM systems, notably in retrieval-augmented generation (RAG), where techniques from information retrieval are used to augment model inference within modular workflows. We propose a behaviour-centric model of system configurations and a unified language for reasoning about such systems. Our framework introduces an intervention operator that captures the notion of *mechanism change*, reflecting interventionist views of causation, while a separation-logic-style conjunction supports local reasoning via explicit system interfaces, consistent with mechanistic accounts that explain phenomena through organized and modifiable parts. Agent policy changes are treated as interventions on the components they control, enabling counterfactual analysis and attribution of responsibility within the same logic. We define actual causation directly in this language and show, via time-unfolding of finite system runs, that our notion aligns with the Halpern-Pearl account of actual causation in the acyclic structural model induced by the run. We establish van Benthem-Hennessy-Milner-style correspondence results: a bisimulation that respects both transitions and interventions characterizes logical equivalence under finiteness assumptions. Thus, we integrate system evolution with modular decomposition within a single language: its modalities refer directly to configuration transitions, interventions on mechanisms, and interface-indexed decompositions. We apply the framework to a retrieval-augmented generation (RAG) workflow for LLM-based systems to specify explicit interfaces, model mechanism changes as interventions, and answer design-time causal queries such as, whether some admissible mechanism change guarantees a stated safety constraint while preserving invariants modularly across an interface.

Keywords: Logic · Transition systems · Distributed systems · Behaviour · Agency · Decision-making · Strategic reasoning · Causality · Interventions · Separation · Large language models · Retrieval-augmented generation

© The Author(s), under exclusive license to Springer Nature Switzerland AG 2026
Y. Mualla et al. (Eds.): CALM 2025, CCIS 2923, pp. 73–95, 2026.
https://doi.org/10.1007/978-3-032-20548-3_6

1   Introduction

Causal reasoning sits at the heart of explanation, control, and design in systems composed of many interacting parts, from software microservice ecosystems [11,30] and cyber-physical controllers to multi-agent LLM workflows and, increasingly, the mechanistic interpretability of neural networks [19]. Practitioners do not only ask *'did X cause Y?'*; instead, they routinely ask *'what* change of mechanism or policy *will* guarantee *or* prevent *Y, while preserving invariants elsewhere?'*. Standard structural causal models provide value-setting interventions on variables, but they do not directly capture mechanism-level changes in modular computational systems, nor do they support reasoning about such changes in a single, compositional logic. This paper develops a logical framework that addresses that design-oriented question with minimal structural assumptions and with an explicit account of *mechanism change* as a first-class intervention. We integrate the logic with system dynamics and modular structure: its modalities speak directly about system transitions and interventions, and it respects a form of van Benthem-Hennessy-Milner correspondence [7].

Standard structural causal models (SCMs), as in the Halpern-Pearl programme [21,35], provide value-setting interventions on variables and underpin a large body of work in causal analysis. In many engineered systems, however, the natural unit of intervention is not a fixed value but a *rule*: a policy switch, a controller update, a threshold change, or a mode transition. Standard structural causal models (SCMs) can encode such régime changes by adding latent 'switch' variables or by moving to a family of models. However, such encodings obscure locality and make it difficult to reason *within a single logic* about *which* mechanism changes are admissible and which invariants they preserve.

Large systems are reasoned about *modularly* on the principle that well-designed interfaces allow change and verification of parts in isolation while preserving global behaviour. Motivated by this, we adopt a behaviour-centric view in which a *system* is a collection of components with observable behaviours; each component updates according to a local rule (mechanism) that depends only on a declared *influence context*. This view characterizes the class of systems we study: discrete-time, locally-interacting computational systems such as process networks, automata or agent-based models, and modular software or ML workflows in which all dependencies are explicit in the influence contexts. Systems whose dynamics rely on intrinsically non-local or hidden global state (for example, centralized schedulers that inspect the entire configuration, or models enforcing global serializability via an implicit transaction log) fall outside our scope. Agents supply policies that feed into these local mechanisms; a policy profile parametrizes the overall dynamics. Most importantly, we treat *interventions* as first-class *mechanism changes*: an intervention rewrites some local rules (policy changes are just a special case). The logic features a single dynamic operator to represent the effect of such an edit and the behaviours reachable afterwards (Sect. 4).

A system may be carved into two regions separated by a 'named' interface that makes dependencies explicit: components on the left may depend on the interface, and components on the right may depend on the interface, but neither side reaches through the interface to the other. This 'boundary' lets us reason locally: a statement about the left side can be checked using only the left-side model (plus the shared interface), and likewise for the right. If we make a mechanism change that is confined to the right side and does not alter the interface, all facts established about the left side at the current configuration continue to hold after the update. The interface functions as a locus of manipulability and control, and provides a means of stable, targeted change emphasized by interventionist accounts of causation [21,40]. We use an *interface-indexed separating conjunction* operator: a statement of the form 'φ on the left and ψ on the right' asserts that φ holds in the model restricted to the left-hand components and ψ holds in the model restricted to the right-hand components, with the two sides sharing only the declared interface. This construction mirrors the locality discipline of logic of bunched implications which enables compositional reasoning about independent parts [34].

We define actual causation (in the sense of Halpern and Pearl [21,22]) directly in our logical language, and by an 'unfolding' construction show that in any finite run of our system models, this notion conforms with Halpern-Pearl actual causes in an acyclic structural model built from that run, with mechanism changes represented as updates to the model itself. The notion of an interface also echoes Causal Influence Diagrams [15,24]: changing a policy corresponds to replacing a decision node's policy. Unlike do-calculus [35] with fixed mechanisms, we reason over a set of admissible mechanism changes: if a change is confined to one side of a declared interface, facts established about the other side still hold. Agent policies fit into this framework as first-class interventions, and coordinated policy changes by multiple agents are just sets of such edits. Practically, this lets causality practitioners pose the design-time questions such as 'is there an admissible mechanism change after which the desired property holds on all continuations?', and obtain a modular safety guarantee.

Taken together, these constructions provide both a notion of correctness and a practical value proposition for the framework. On the one hand, the time-unfolding alignment result shows that, for any finite run of a system in our sense, the actual-cause relation defined in our logic coincides with Halpern-Pearl actual causation in a canonically associated acyclic SCM. In particular, all standard HP-style causal judgements are preserved when we move from structural equations to our behaviour-centric, mechanism-changing view. On the other hand, the interface discipline and separating conjunction give a modular account of *where* and *how* mechanisms may be changed without invalidating previously established properties. This supports design-oriented questions of the form: *"Is there an admissible mechanism change, confined to this subsystem, after which the desired property holds on all continuations, while invariants elsewhere are preserved?"* In our instantiation to agentic RAG-LLM workflows (Sect. 6), these questions correspond to concrete design and debugging tasks. Examples include isolating whether retrieval, ranking, or generation mechanisms must be altered to eliminate a class of failures.

In summary, our contributions are: (i) a behaviour-centric system model with explicit influence contexts and mechanism-changing interventions; (ii) a modal logic $\mathcal{L}(\langle\theta\rangle,*_\Lambda)$ for reasoning about such interventions and interfaces; (iii) a notion of actual causation that is provably aligned with Halpern-Pearl actual causation on finite runs; and (iv) an instantiation to agentic RAG-LLM workflows illustrating modular, design-oriented causal reasoning.

Section 2 introduces the behaviour-centric system model, interfaces, interventions, and system decompositions. Section 3 adds agents and policy profiles, and shows how policy changes are represented as interventions. Section 4 presents the logic $\mathcal{L}(\langle\theta\rangle,*_\Lambda)$ and its semantics on restricted models. Section 5 defines actual causation and establishes its alignment with the Halpern-Pearl framework via a time-unfolding construction. Section 6 instantiates the framework on representative systems, focusing on agentic RAG-LLM workflows. Section 7 develops an intervention-preserving bisimulation and proves soundness and completeness. Section 8 reflects on philosophical motivations, summarizes limitations, and sketches quantitative extensions.

2   The System Modelling Framework

In this section, we adopt a deliberately minimalist, behaviour-centric view of systems: instead of enumerating internal state, a component is specified by the *behaviours* an external observer can witness and by how those behaviours *influence* other components. This draws a line between intensional state (irrelevant here) and extensional behaviour (observable facts). This point of view, introduced in [17], represents a more abstract view of models of distributed systems than that based on process calculus and process logic as introduced in, for example, [3,9,10], building on a body of earlier work cited therein. Also refer to [13] for a related perspective, and to [38] for a historical background.

In particular, we now fix our scope. Although the framework is expressive enough to encode components with arbitrarily large influence contexts, our intended domain is *discrete-time, locally-interacting computational systems*. These are systems in which (i) there is a distinguished set of components $\mathcal{C}$, (ii) each component exposes observable behaviours $\mathbb{B}(c)$, and (iii) component updates depend only on behaviours in a declared *influence context* $\mathsf{Inf}(c)$. This captures a broad class of models in informatics, including automata and agent networks, process and microservice graphs, and modular LLM workflows, among many others, provided that all dependencies are explicit in $\mathsf{Inf}(\cdot)$. Formally, one could represent a globally-coupled subsystem (such as a central scheduler that inspects the entire configuration, or a transactional layer enforcing global serializability via an implicit log), as a single 'mega-component' with a global influence context. However, such encodings violate the *locality discipline* that underpins our interface and compositionality results (cf. Sect. 7).

This section is devoted to the base behavioural model of system evolution; in Sect. 3 we discuss agents and policies. Formally, let $\mathcal{C}$ be the set of components and $\mathcal{B}$ the set of all behaviours. A mapping $\mathbb{B} : \mathcal{C} \rightarrow 2^{\mathcal{B}}$ assigns to each $c \in \mathcal{C}$

its allowable behaviours $\mathbb{B}(c)$. A *configuration* specifies the current behaviour of every component (cf. [13] for a similar theme).

Definition 1 (Configuration). *A* configuration *over $\mathcal{C}$ is a total function $f : \mathcal{C} \to \mathcal{B}$ with $f(c) \in \mathbb{B}(c)$ for all $c \in \mathcal{C}$. The set of all configurations is $F_{\mathcal{C}}$; when $\mathcal{C}$ is clear we write F.* □

To model evolution we use *influence mechanisms*: for each component, a function that, given its current behaviour and the behaviours of selected others, returns its next behaviour.

Definition 2 (Influence mechanisms and contexts). *For each $c \in \mathcal{C}$, the* influence context $\mathsf{Inf}(c) \subseteq \mathcal{C} \setminus \{c\}$ *lists those components whose behaviours are relevant for updating c. An* influence mechanism *for c is a function $\mathcal{I}_c : \mathbb{B}(c) \times \prod_{d \in \mathsf{Inf}(c)} \mathbb{B}(d) \to \mathbb{B}(c)$. The set $\mathcal{I} = \{\mathcal{I}_c\}_{c \in \mathcal{C}}$ denotes all such mechanisms.* □

Definition 3 (Transition relation). *Given $(\mathcal{C}, \mathbb{B}, \mathcal{I})$, the* transition relation *$\Delta_{\mathcal{I}} \subseteq F \times F$ contains (f, f') iff there exists exactly one $c \in \mathcal{C}$ such that $f'(c) = \mathcal{I}_c(f(c), (f(d))_{d \in \mathsf{Inf}(c)})$ and for all, $d \neq c$: $f'(d) = f(d)$. Thus, each step updates precisely one component according to its corresponding mechanism.* □

Remark 1. The one-component update discipline in Definition 3 is a modelling choice rather than a limitation: synchronous or multi-component updates can be represented by packing several basic components into a compound component with a joint mechanism. We work with the simpler asynchronous presentation because it makes locality and interfaces more transparent. □

Definition 4 (System model). *A* system model *is $\mathcal{M} = (\mathcal{C}, \mathcal{B}, \mathcal{I}, F, \Delta_{\mathcal{I}}, \Gamma)$, where F and $\Delta_{\mathcal{I}}$ are as above, and $\Gamma : \mathcal{P} \to 2^F$ is a valuation assigning to each atomic proposition the set of configurations where it holds. For brevity we often write $\mathcal{M} = (F, \Delta_{\mathcal{I}}, \Gamma)$.* □

Example 1. Let $\mathcal{C} = \{c_1, c_2, c_3\}$ with $\mathbb{B}(c_1) = \{b_{11}, b_{12}, b_{13}\}$, $\mathbb{B}(c_2) = \{b_{21}, b_{22}\}$, $\mathbb{B}(c_3) = \{b_{31}\}$. Take $\mathsf{Inf}(c_1) = \varnothing$, $\mathsf{Inf}(c_2) = \{c_1\}$, $\mathsf{Inf}(c_3) = \varnothing$, and mechanisms $\mathcal{I}_{c_1}(b_{11}) = b_{12}$, $\mathcal{I}_{c_1}(b_{12}) = b_{13}$, $\mathcal{I}_{c_1}(b_{13}) = b_{11}$, $\mathcal{I}_{c_2}(b_{21}, b_{12}) = b_{22}$, $\mathcal{I}_{c_2}(b_{21}, \_) = b_{21}$, $\mathcal{I}_{c_2}(b_{22}, \_) = b_{22}$, $\mathcal{I}_{c_3}(b_{31}) = b_{31}$. Let f_1 be a configuration such that $f_1(c_1) = b_{11}, f_1(c_2) = b_{21}, f_1(c_3) = b_{31}$. Then updating c_1 yields f_2 with $f_2(c_1) = b_{12}$ and $f_2(c_2) = b_{21}, f_2(c_3) = b_{31}$, so $(f_1, f_2) \in \Delta_{\mathcal{I}}$. □

To analyse subsystems, we use partial configurations and an *interface* that mediates dependencies across a decomposition.

Definition 5 (Partial configuration). *If $\mathcal{C}' \subseteq \mathcal{C}$, a partial configuration* over *$\mathcal{C}'$ is a function $f' : \mathcal{C}' \to \bigcup_{c \in \mathcal{C}'} \mathbb{B}(c)$ with $f'(c) \in \mathbb{B}(c)$. The restriction of $f \in F$ to $\mathcal{C}'$ is $f{\restriction}_{\mathcal{C}'}$.* □

Definition 6 (Admissible interface-cut). *Let $\mathcal{M}$ have component set $\mathcal{C}$ and influence map $\mathsf{Inf}(\cdot)$. A triple (C_1, I, C_2) with $C_1 \cup C_2 = \mathcal{C}$ and $I = C_1 \cap C_2$ is an* admissible interface-cut *iff the following conditions are satisfied:*

1. (**Left locality**) *For all $c \in C_1 \setminus I$, $\mathsf{Inf}(c) \subseteq C_1 \cup I$.*
2. (**Right locality**) *For all $c \in C_2 \setminus I$, $\mathsf{Inf}(c) \subseteq C_2 \cup I$.*
3. (**Interface closure**) *For all $c \in I$, $\mathsf{Inf}(c) \subseteq I$.*

A model is interface-admitting *if it admits at least one interface-cut.* $\square$

Remark 2. For each $c \in C_i$, one may view $\mathcal{I}_c$ as a local mechanism $\mathcal{I}_c^i$ over $C_i \cup I$ (the two coincide on shared inputs). $\square$

Example 2 (Interface). With the contexts and mechanisms from Example 1, take $C_1 = \{c_1, c_2\}$, $C_2 = \{c_1, c_3\}$, and $I = C_1 \cap C_2 = \{c_1\}$. Then the three interface conditions hold, so $\{c_1\}$ is an interface. $\square$

Definition 7 (Restriction along a cut). *Fix an admissible interface-cut $\lambda = (C_1, I, C_2)$ in a system model $\mathcal{M}$. For $j \in \{1,2\}$, the C_j-restriction $\mathcal{M}\!\restriction_{C_j}$ is the system model obtained by: keeping only components in C_j; and, restricting behaviours and configurations to C_j; and, inducing a transition relation on C_j from $\Delta_{\mathcal{I}}$; that is, $f_j \Delta_{C_j}^{\lambda} f_j'$ iff there exist f, f' in $\mathcal{M}$ with $f \Delta_{\mathcal{I}} f'$, $f\!\restriction_{C_j} = f_j$, $f'\!\restriction_{C_j} = f_j'$, and $f'\!\restriction_I = f\!\restriction_I$. By locality and interface-closure in Definition 6, $\mathcal{M}\!\restriction_{C_j}$ is well-defined. Moreover, if $f \Delta_{\mathcal{I}} f'$ in $\mathcal{M}$, then for $j = 1, 2$, $f\!\restriction_{C_j} \Delta_{C_j}^{\lambda} f'\!\restriction_{C_j}$ and $f'\!\restriction_I = f\!\restriction_I$.* $\square$

Interventions replace (some of) the right-hand sides of the influence mechanisms while preserving the input contexts $\mathsf{Inf}(c)$.

Definition 8 (Intervention payload). *Given a model $\mathcal{M}$, for a component c, let $\mathsf{Inp}(c) := \prod_{d \in \mathsf{Inf}(c)} \mathbb{B}(d)$. An intervention payload is a pair $(T, \mathcal{J}_T)$ where $T \subseteq \mathcal{C}$ and $\mathcal{J}_T = \{\mathcal{J}_c : \mathbb{B}(c) \times \mathsf{Inp}(c) \to \mathbb{B}(c)_{c \in T}$ provides replacement mechanisms for exactly the targets in T. Applying $(T, \mathcal{J}_T)$ to an augmented model $\mathcal{M}$ yields $\mathcal{M}[T \mapsto \mathcal{J}_T]$, which keeps $\mathcal{C}$, $\mathbb{B}$, $\mathsf{Inf}(\cdot)$, F, and Γ unchanged; and replaces $\mathcal{I}_c$ by $\mathcal{J}_c$ for $c \in T$, leaving $\mathcal{I}_c$ unchanged for $c \notin T$, with the transition relation recomputed from the modified family of mechanisms. If θ denotes an intervention, we write $\mathcal{M}_\theta = \mathcal{M}[T \mapsto \mathcal{J}_T]$.* $\square$

Example 3. In Example 1, let $\theta = (\{c_1\}, \{\mathcal{I}_{c_1}'\})$ be an such that $\mathcal{I}_{c_1}'(b_{11}) = \mathcal{I}_{c_1}'(b_{12}) = \mathcal{I}_{c_1}'(b_{13}) = b_{11}$. In the intervened model $\mathcal{M}_\theta$, every reachable configuration f satisfies $f(c_1) = b_{11}$; consequently c_2 remains at b_{21}. $\square$

Remark 3. If $\mathcal{M}$ is interface-admitting and θ is *cut-preserving* i.e., it leaves all influence contexts unchanged and does not rewrite the mechanisms of any interface component of any admissible interface-cut, then every interface-cut (C_1, I, C_2) admissible in $\mathcal{M}$ remains admissible in $\mathcal{M}_\theta$; in particular, $\mathcal{M}_\theta$ admits the same (C_1, I, C_2). $\square$

Definition 9 (Augmented model). *An* augmented model *is a tuple $\widehat{\mathcal{M}} = (\mathcal{C}, \mathbb{B}, \mathcal{I}, F, \Delta_{\mathcal{I}}, \Gamma, \mathsf{cut}, \llbracket \cdot \rrbracket)$, where the first six components form a system model, $\mathsf{cut} : \Lambda \to \{(C_1, I, C_2)\}$ assigns admissible interface-cuts (Definition 6), and $\llbracket \cdot \rrbracket$ interprets each label θ by installing the corresponding intervention payload (Definition 8) and updating the induced transition relation.* $\square$

3 Agents and Agency

Many systems are steered by decision makers whose choices are best viewed as *policy changes* to parts of the mechanism. Our goal is to reason about questions such as: what if an actor switches policy, which edits guarantee a safety property, and how should responsibility be attributed? We keep agency lightweight and compatible with the existing intervention modality, rather than introducing a separate strategic calculus (see [1] for an alternative approach).

Closer to work at the interface of causality and multi-agent systems, Gladyshev, Alechina, Dastani and Doder use Halpern-Pearl causal models to represent organisational decision dependencies and derive a concurrent game structure in which agents can intervene on their local part of the causal model to change dependencies [20]. Their framework combines SCMs with CGS semantics to study strategic abilities and responsibility. In contrast, we start from behaviour-centric transition systems with local influence mechanisms and interfaces, internalize interventions as a dynamic modality in the object language, and obtain HP-aligned actual causation via a time-unfolding construction rather than via a direct SCM-to-CGS embedding.

Agents and Policies: Let $\widehat{\mathcal{M}} = (\mathcal{C}, \mathbb{B}, \mathcal{I}, F, \Delta_{\mathcal{I}}, \Gamma,\ \mathrm{cut},\ [\![\cdot]\!])$ be an augmented model, and let $\mathcal{A}$ be a finite set of agents. For each component $c \in \mathcal{C}$, write $A_c \subseteq \mathcal{A}$ for the agents that are permitted to change c's mechanism, and for each agent a let $C_a := \{\, c \in \mathcal{C} \mid a \in A_c \,\}$ be the set of components controlled by a. For simplicity, we assume each component is controlled by at most one agent, so the sets C_a form a partial partition of $\mathcal{C}$.

A *policy choice* by an agent can be viewed as selecting, from a set of admissible replacements, new mechanisms for the components it controls. We fix, for each $c \in \mathcal{C}$, a set of admissible local influence mechanisms $\mathrm{Adm}(c) \subseteq \{\mathcal{J}_c : \mathbb{B}(c) \times \prod_{d \in \mathsf{Inf}(c)} \mathbb{B}(d) \to \mathbb{B}(c)\}$, required to respect locality (depend only on $\mathsf{Inf}(c)$). In particular, each admissible mechanism $\mathcal{J}_c$ has input type $\mathrm{Inp}(c) = \prod_{d \in \mathsf{Inf}(c)} \mathbb{B}(d)$ and depends only on $\mathsf{Inf}(c)$. Concretely, for a coalition $A \subseteq \mathcal{A}$, a joint policy change is an intervention payload $(T, \mathcal{J}_T)$ with $T \subseteq \bigcup_{a \in A} C_a$,

$$\mathcal{J}_T = \{\mathcal{J}_c \in \mathrm{Adm}(c) \mid c \in T\}.$$

Remark 4. We restrict attention to systems in which each component is controlled by at most one agent at a time, so that the sets C_a form a partial partition of $\mathcal{C}$. This avoids the need to specify a separate conflict-resolution semantics for the case where multiple agents propose incompatible mechanisms for the same component. The restriction is not substantial: coordinated or competitive decision-making by several agents can be modelled by inserting an additional 'controller' component upstream, whose behaviour aggregates their choices and is itself controlled by a single (possibly coalitional) agent. From the point of view of the underlying transition system and the causal notions developed later, this single-controller discipline preserves expressiveness while simplifying both the operational semantics and responsibility attribution. □

Definition 10 (Policy profile). *A policy profile is a family $\Pi = \{\Pi_a \mid a \in \mathcal{A}\}$ such that each Π_a assigns, to every $c \in C_a$, a mechanism $\Pi_a(c) \in \mathrm{Adm}(c)$. The mechanism in force at c under Π is*

$$\mathcal{I}_c^\Pi = \begin{cases} \Pi_a(c) & \textit{if there exists an agent } a \textit{ with } c \in C_a, \\ \mathcal{I}_c & \textit{otherwise.} \end{cases}$$

$\square$

Definition 11 (Policy intervention). *Given a coalition $A \subseteq \mathcal{A}$ and a finite target set $T \subseteq \bigcup_{a \in A} C_a$ with replacement mechanisms $\mathcal{J}_T = \{\mathcal{J}_c \in \mathrm{Adm}(c) \mid c \in T\}$, the policy intervention $\theta_{A,\mathcal{J}_T}$ has interpretation $[\![\theta_{A,\mathcal{J}_T}]\!](\widehat{\mathcal{M}}, \Pi) = (\widehat{\mathcal{M}}[T \mapsto \mathcal{J}_T], \Pi_\theta)$. Here, $\widehat{\mathcal{M}}[T \mapsto \mathcal{J}_T]$ rewrites the local mechanisms for $c \in T$ to $\mathcal{J}_c$, and the updated policy profile Π_θ is obtained by overriding the components controlled by agents in A so that, for each $a \in A$ and $c \in C_a$,*

$$\Pi_\theta(a)(c) = \begin{cases} \mathcal{J}_c & \textit{if } c \in T, \\ \Pi_a(c) & \textit{otherwise.} \end{cases}$$

For non-policy (pure) interventions we set $\Pi_\theta := \Pi$. $\square$

Definition 12 (Transition relation under a policy). *Fix an augmented model $\widehat{\mathcal{M}} = (\mathcal{C}, \mathbb{B}, \mathcal{I}, F, \Delta_\mathcal{I}, \Gamma, \mathsf{cut}, [\![\cdot]\!])$ and a policy profile Π. Let $\mathcal{I}^\Pi = \{\mathcal{I}_c^\Pi\}_{c \in \mathcal{C}}$ be the family of local mechanisms in force under Π (Definition 10). The transition relation induced by Π is the relation $\Delta_{\mathcal{I}^\Pi} \subseteq F \times F$ defined by $f \Delta_{\mathcal{I}^\Pi} f'$ iff there exists $c \in \mathcal{C}$ such that $f'(c) = \mathcal{I}_c^\Pi\big(f(c), (f(d))_{d \in \mathsf{Inf}(c)}\big)$ and $f'(d) = f(d)$ for all $d \neq c$.*

If an intervention θ has interpretation $[\![\theta]\!](\widehat{\mathcal{M}}, \Pi) = (\widehat{\mathcal{M}}_\theta, \Pi_\theta)$ with updated mechanisms $\mathcal{I}_\theta$ in $\widehat{\mathcal{M}}_\theta$ (Definition 11), let $\mathcal{I}_\theta^{\Pi_\theta}$ be the family of mechanisms in force in $\widehat{\mathcal{M}}_\theta$ under Π_θ, obtained by applying Definition 10 with base mechanisms $\mathcal{I}_\theta$ and profile Π_θ. Post-intervention transition steps are then taken with respect to $\Delta_{\mathcal{I}_\theta^{\Pi_\theta}}$. $\square$

4   Syntax and Semantics

4.1   Syntax

Let $\mathcal{P}$ be a denumerable set of atomic propositions. Fix two denumerable sets of *labels*, Θ (symbols naming admissible interventions), ranged over by θ, and Λ (symbols naming admissible interface-cuts), ranged over by λ. The language $\mathcal{L}(\langle\theta\rangle, *_\Lambda)$ is generated by:

$$\varphi ::= p \mid \neg\varphi \mid \varphi \wedge \varphi \mid \Box\varphi \mid \Diamond\varphi \mid \langle\theta\rangle\varphi \mid \varphi *_\lambda \psi,$$

where $p \in \mathcal{P}$, $\theta \in \Theta$, and $\lambda \in \Lambda$. As usual, $\varphi \vee \psi$, $\varphi \to \psi$, and $\top, \bot$ are defined classically. We write $\Diamond^+\varphi$ (resp. $\Box^+\varphi$) as shorthand for the existential (resp. universal) modality over the transitive closure of the transition relation (see semantics).

4.2 Semantics

We work with augmented models (Definition 9) $\widehat{\mathcal{M}} = (\mathcal{C}, \mathbb{B}, \mathcal{I}, F, \Delta_{\mathcal{I}}, \Gamma, \mathsf{cut}, [\![\cdot]\!])$, where $\mathsf{cut} : \Lambda \to \{(C_1, I, C_2) \mid C_1 \cup C_2 = \mathcal{C},\ I = C_1 \cap C_2\}$ selects admissible interface-cuts, and $[\![\cdot]\!]$ interprets each intervention label $\theta \in \Theta$ as a mechanism-change operator. Given an augmented model and a policy profile $(\widehat{\mathcal{M}}, \Pi)$, we write $[\![\theta]\!](\widehat{\mathcal{M}}, \Pi) = (\widehat{\mathcal{M}}_\theta, \Pi_\theta)$, where $\widehat{\mathcal{M}}_\theta = (\mathcal{C}, \mathbb{B}, \mathcal{I}_\theta, F, \Delta_{\mathcal{I}_\theta}, \Gamma, \mathsf{cut}, [\![\cdot]\!])$ is obtained by installing the replacement mechanisms (Definition 8) and Π_θ is the updated policy profile (Definition 11).

Definition 13. *Satisfaction* $(\widehat{\mathcal{M}}, f, \Pi) \models \varphi$ *is defined by*

$$
\begin{aligned}
(\widehat{\mathcal{M}}, f, \Pi) &\models p && \textit{iff } f \in \Gamma(p) \\
(\widehat{\mathcal{M}}, f, \Pi) &\models \neg\varphi && \textit{iff } (\widehat{\mathcal{M}}, f, \Pi) \not\models \varphi \\
(\widehat{\mathcal{M}}, f, \Pi) &\models \varphi \wedge \psi && \textit{iff } (\widehat{\mathcal{M}}, f, \Pi) \models \varphi \textit{ and } (\widehat{\mathcal{M}}, f, \Pi) \models \psi \\
(\widehat{\mathcal{M}}, f, \Pi) &\models \Diamond\varphi && \textit{iff } \textit{for some } f' \in F \textit{ s.t. } (f\ \Delta_{\mathcal{I}\Pi}\ f' \textit{ and } (\widehat{\mathcal{M}}, f', \Pi) \models \varphi) \\
(\widehat{\mathcal{M}}, f, \Pi) &\models \Box\varphi && \textit{iff } \textit{for all } f' \in F \textit{ s.t. } (f\ \Delta_{\mathcal{I}\Pi}\ f' \textit{ implies } (\widehat{\mathcal{M}}, f', \Pi) \models \varphi) \\
(\widehat{\mathcal{M}}, f, \Pi) &\models \langle\theta\rangle\varphi && \textit{iff } \textit{for some } f' \in F \textit{ s.t.} \\
&&& \quad (\ [\![\theta]\!](\widehat{\mathcal{M}}, \Pi) = (\widehat{\mathcal{M}}_\theta, \Pi_\theta), \\
&&& \quad\ f\,(\Delta_{\mathcal{I}_\theta \Pi_\theta})^\star f', \textit{ and } (\widehat{\mathcal{M}}_\theta, f', \Pi_\theta) \models \varphi) \\
(\widehat{\mathcal{M}}, f, \Pi) &\models \varphi *_\lambda \psi && \textit{iff } (C_1, I, C_2) \textit{ is an admissible interface-cut in } \widehat{\mathcal{M}} \textit{ and} \\
&&& \quad (\widehat{\mathcal{M}}{\restriction}_{C_1}, f{\restriction}_{C_1}, \Pi) \models \varphi \textit{ and } (\widehat{\mathcal{M}}{\restriction}_{C_2}, f{\restriction}_{C_2}, \Pi) \models \psi
\end{aligned}
$$

Here $R^\star$ (and R^+ below) denote the reflexivetransitive (resp. transitive) closure of a binary relation R. We write $\Diamond^+\varphi$ (resp. $\Box^+\varphi$) as shorthand for the existential (resp. universal) modality over the transitive closure $(\Delta_{\mathcal{I}\Pi})^+$. $\qquad\square$

For $C' \subseteq \mathcal{C}$, we write $\widehat{\mathcal{M}}{\restriction}_{C'} = (C', \mathbb{B}{\restriction}_{C'}, \mathcal{I}{\restriction}_{C'}, F_{C'}, \Delta^{C'}, \Gamma{\restriction}_{C'}, \mathsf{cut}{\restriction}_{C'}, [\![\cdot]\!])$ where $F_{C'}$ is the set of partial configurations $g : C' \to \bigcup_{c \in C'} \mathbb{B}(c)$ with $g(c) \in \mathbb{B}(c)$; and, $\Gamma{\restriction}_{C'}(p) = \{g \in F_{C'} \mid \text{for some } f \in \Gamma(p) \text{ with } f{\restriction}_{C'} = g\}$ (valuation restricted to C'), and, $\Delta^{C'} \subseteq F_{C'} \times F_{C'}$ is given by $(g, g') \in \Delta^{C'}$ iff, for some $f, f' \in F$, $f{\restriction}_{C'} = g, f'{\restriction}_{C'} = g', (f, f') \in \Delta_{\mathcal{I}}$. When we evaluate satisfaction in a restricted model under a profile Π, we implicitly use the restriction of $\Delta_{\mathcal{I}\Pi}$ to C' in place of $\Delta_{\mathcal{I}}$.

When $\lambda = (C_1, I, C_2)$ is admissible, the restricted relation $\Delta^\lambda_{C_i}$ coincides with the transition obtained by executing only the local mechanisms on C_i while keeping the interface I fixed; this follows from left/right locality and interface-closure (Definition 6), and therefore satisfaction in $\widehat{\mathcal{M}}{\restriction}_{C_i}$ is well-defined. Under agent policy interventions (Sect. 3), replacement influence mechanisms for any c depend only on $\mathsf{Inf}(c)$ and no mechanism for components in I is altered.

5 Actual Causation in System Models

Halpern-Pearl structural causal models (SCMs) [21,35] represent a scenario by endogenous variables V, an exogenous context U, and structural equations F

that determine each V_i from its parents. Interventions are value-setting changes $\mathrm{do}(X = x)$ that replace the equation for X and induce counterfactual worlds. HP define *actual cause* of an effect ψ_E via three clauses: (AC1) *actuality* ($X = x$ and ψ_E both hold), (AC2) *counterfactual dependence under a contingency* (there exists W such that $[X \leftarrow x', W \leftarrow w] \neg\psi_E$), and (AC3) *minimality*. SCMs excel at post-hoc analysis, but design-time reasoning about *which* mechanism changes are admissible and *where* they apply often forces one to move across families of models or to introduce ad-hoc switch variables.

Philosophically, our choice to treat *mechanism change* as the core intervention aligns with manipulability accounts of causation: causes are what can be purposefully changed to control effects. In engineered, multiagent settings the natural unit of manipulation is rarely a variable-value assignment but a *rule edit*. Making such edits first-class situates the logic at the level of design and control, not merely post-hoc explanation. Viewing agent's policies as interventions matches the agency-as-capacity-to-intervene view: agents have an admissible policy set over its observations. A *choice* by the agent is represented by an intervention whose interpretation updates exactly the mechanisms for those components it can control. This matches interventionist accounts of causation, where control is analysed via counterfactual changes one can *bring about* [40], and it is conformant with mechanistic views that explain phenomena by operations of organized parts and their modifiable activities [32,38].

Another closely related formalism is that of Causal Influence Diagrams which extend classical influence diagrams with a causal interpretation of arcs, combining chance, decision, and utility nodes within a single directed acyclic graph and supporting counterfactual reasoning via Pearl's do-calculus [24,35,37]. Recent work extends CIDs to agent modelling, sequential decision-making, and safety analysis in multi-agent systems [15,23,29]. In contrast, our framework treats both *mechanistic* and *policy-induced* changes uniformly through a single intervention modality $\langle\theta\rangle\varphi$, interpreted directly in the transition semantics.

We define an actual cause as follows:

Definition 14 (Actual cause). *Let $f_0, f_1 \in F$ be configurations, and let the effect be a formula ψ_E whose atoms lie in a designated set $C_E \subseteq C$. A non-empty set of components $C^\star \subseteq C$ is an* actual cause *of $(\widehat{\mathcal{M}}, f_1, \Pi) \models \psi_E$ from f_0 (written $\mathrm{Cause}_\Pi(f_0, f_1; C^\star, \psi_E)$) iff the following hold:*

(AC1) Actuality: $(\widehat{\mathcal{M}}, f_1, \Pi) \models \psi_E \wedge \chi_{C^\star}(f_0)$ *and* $f_0\,(\Delta_{\mathcal{I}\Pi})^+\,f_1$.

(AC2^m) Counterfactual dependence with witness: There exists a witness set $W \subseteq C$, an admissible interface-cut $\lambda = (C_1, I, C_2)$,[1] and an intervention label $\theta \in \Theta$ such that $(\widehat{\mathcal{M}}, f_0, \Pi) \models \langle\theta\rangle\,(\chi_W(f_0) *_\lambda \delta_{C^\star \setminus W}(f_0) \wedge \Box^+\neg(\psi_E \wedge \chi_{C^\star}(f_0)))$. Intuitively, there is an admissible intervention θ and a post-intervention configuration reachable from f_0 in which the components in W remain as in f_0 while at least one coordinate in $C^\star \setminus W$ is changed, and from that configuration all continuations fail to realize ψ_E together with $\chi_{C^\star}(f_0)$.

---

[1] For example, take $W \subseteq C_1$ and $(C^\star \setminus W) \subseteq C_2$ so that $\chi_W(f_0)$ and $\delta_{C^\star \setminus W}(f_0)$ can be conjoined via $*_\lambda$.

(AC3) Minimality *No proper subset $C' \subsetneq C^\star$ satisfies $\boldsymbol{AC1}$ and $\boldsymbol{AC2^m}$ with the same f_0, f_1 and some (possibly different) W, λ, θ.* $\square$

5.1 HP-Alignment

Our notions (Definition 14) are aligned with the Halpern-Pearl framework in the following sense: for any finite evolution, we can build a *time-unfolded* structural causal model (SCM) whose variables are the components in our system indexed by discrete steps. This yields an acyclic SCM suitable for defining standard HP actual causation [21,22]. The construction is analogous to the familiar unrolling of dynamic or feedback systems into time-indexed acyclic graphical models, as used for dynamic Bayesian networks and temporal probabilistic reasoning [28, 35].

We first associate a 'time-unfolded' SCM to a finite run of the system model. Fix a policy profile Π and a finite sequence of configurations $(f_0, \ldots, f_n)$ with $f_i \, \Delta_{\mathcal{I}^\Pi} \, f_{i+1}$ for $i = 0, \ldots, n-1$, so that exactly one component is updated at each step. Let $(s_1, \ldots, s_n)$ be the (deterministic) choice of updating components, where $s_i \in \mathcal{C}$ is the unique component updated at the i-th step. Define the SCM $M_{\mathrm{unf}}(n, \Pi) = \langle U, V, F \rangle$ as follows:

1. Endogenous variables $V = \{V_c^i \mid c \in \mathcal{C}, i = 0, \ldots, n\}$, with $\mathrm{dom}(V_c^i) = \mathbb{B}(c)$.
2. Exogenous variables $U = \{U_0, \ S^1, \ldots, S^n\}$, where U_0 fixes the initial configuration and each S^i is a scheduler selecting s_i.
3. Structural functions F:

$$V_c^0 = f_0(c) \qquad \text{(determined by } U_0\text{)},$$

$$V_c^i = \begin{cases} \mathcal{I}_c^\Pi(V_c^{i-1}, \ (V_d^{i-1})_{d \in \mathsf{Inf}(c)}) & \text{if } S^i = c, \\ V_c^{i-1} & \text{if } S^i \neq c, \end{cases} \qquad i = 1, \ldots, n.$$

This graph is acyclic (edges point from time $i-1$ to i) and has a unique solution for any context $\boldsymbol{u} = (U_0 = f_0, \ S^i = s_i)$, namely $V_c^i = f_i(c)$.

Interventions can be viewed as changes of model. A mechanism or policy intervention $\theta \in \Theta$ that (possibly) rewrites the influence mechanisms for a subset $S_\theta \subseteq \mathcal{C}$ induces a *modified* unfolded SCM $M_{\mathrm{unf}}^\theta(n, \Pi)$ by replacing, for all $c \in S_\theta$ and all $i \geq 1$, the right-hand side $\mathcal{I}_c^\Pi(\cdots)$ with the post-intervention mechanism $\mathcal{I}_c^{\Pi_\theta}(\cdots)$; all other equations remain unchanged. This mirrors our semantics where $(\widehat{\mathcal{M}}, \Pi)$ is mapped to $(\widehat{\mathcal{M}}_\theta, \Pi_\theta)$ before taking (reflexive-transitive) steps.

Theorem 1 (HP-alignment). *Let $(f_0, \ldots, f_n)$ be a causal chain in $(\widehat{\mathcal{M}}, \Pi)$ with outcome f_n and let ψ_E be an effect formula whose atoms lie in $C_E \subseteq \mathcal{C}$. Suppose $C^\star \subseteq \mathcal{C}$ is an actual cause of ψ_E from f_0 to f_n in the sense of Definition 14, witnessed by (W, λ, θ) for $\boldsymbol{AC2^m}$. Define the unfolded SCM $M_{\mathrm{unf}}(n, \Pi)$ and the effect formula $\varphi_E^n := \bigwedge_{c \in C_E}(V_c^n = f_n(c))$. Let $X := \{V_c^0 \mid c \in C^\star\}$ and $x := (f_0(c))_{c \in C^\star}$. Then there exists a context $\boldsymbol{u}$ (namely $U_0 = f_0$ and the schedule realizing the chain) such that, in the HP sense:*

*(1) **AC1**. $(M_{\mathrm{unf}}(n, \Pi), \boldsymbol{u}) \models (X{=}x) \wedge \varphi_E^n$.*
*(2) **AC2**. There is a (possibly empty) set $W' \subseteq V$ of time-0 variables (namely $W' = \{V_c^0 \mid c \in W\}$ encoding the witness W initially) and an assignment w^* to W' that fixes each $V_c^0 \in W'$ to its f_0-value in $\boldsymbol{u}$ such that, in the modified model $M_{\mathrm{unf}}^\theta(n, \Pi)$,*

$$(M_{\mathrm{unf}}^\theta(n, \Pi), \boldsymbol{u}) \models \big[X \leftarrow x', \ W' \leftarrow w^*\big]\neg\varphi_E^n$$

for some x' differing from x on at least one coordinate (corresponding to $\delta_{C^* \setminus W}(f_0)$).
*(3) **AC3**. X is minimal for AC1–AC2 above.*

Hence $X{=}x$ is an HP actual cause of φ_E^n in the unfolded model.

Proof. We proceed in three steps, corresponding to HP's **AC1–AC3**.

We first show the correctness of the unfolding. Fix a policy profile Π and a finite run $(f_0, \ldots, f_n)$ with $f_i \, \Delta_{\mathcal{I}^\Pi} \, f_{i+1}$ for $i = 0, \ldots, n-1$, so that exactly one component is updated at each step. Let $(s_1, \ldots, s_n)$ be the corresponding sequence of updating components, where $s_i \in \mathcal{C}$ is the unique component updated at the i-th step. Consider the SCM $M_{\mathrm{unf}}(n, \Pi) = \langle U, V, F \rangle$ defined as in Sect. 5.1, and the context $\boldsymbol{u} = (U_0 = f_0, \ S^1 = s_1, \ldots, S^n = s_n)$. We claim that under this context the unique solution of $M_{\mathrm{unf}}(n, \Pi)$ satisfies $V_c^i = f_i(c)$ for all $c \in \mathcal{C}$ and $i = 0, \ldots, n$. We prove by induction on i. By definition of F, $V_c^0 = f_0(c)$ for all c, determined directly by $U_0 = f_0$. Thus $V_c^0 = f_0(c)$ for all $c \in \mathcal{C}$.

Inductive step: Assume for some $i-1$ with $1 \leq i \leq n$, $V_c^{i-1} = f_{i-1}(c)$ for all c. By construction of the SCM, for each c we have

$$V_c^i = \begin{cases} \mathcal{I}_c^\Pi(V_c^{i-1}, \ (V_d^{i-1})_{d \in \mathsf{Inf}(c)}) & \text{if } S^i = c, \\ V_c^{i-1} & \text{if } S^i \neq c. \end{cases}$$

Under the context $\boldsymbol{u}$, $S^i = s_i$. By definition of the transition relation $\Delta_{\mathcal{I}^\Pi}$, the step $f_{i-1} \Delta_{\mathcal{I}^\Pi} f_i$ is realized by updating exactly the component s_i, i.e., $f_i(s_i) = \mathcal{I}_{s_i}^\Pi(f_{i-1}(s_i), \ (f_{i-1}(d))_{d \in \mathsf{Inf}(s_i)})$, and $f_i(d) = f_{i-1}(d)$ for all $d \neq s_i$. Using the induction hypothesis $V_c^{i-1} = f_{i-1}(c)$ for all c, we obtain $V_{s_i}^i = \mathcal{I}_{s_i}^\Pi(V_{s_i}^{i-1}, \ (V_d^{i-1})_{d \in \mathsf{Inf}(s_i)}) = \mathcal{I}_{s_i}^\Pi(f_{i-1}(s_i), \ (f_{i-1}(d))_{d \in \mathsf{Inf}(s_i)}) = f_i(s_i)$, and for $d \neq s_i$, $V_d^i = V_d^{i-1} = f_{i-1}(d) = f_i(d)$. Thus $V_c^i = f_i(c)$ for all c, completing the induction. Uniqueness follows from the functional form of the structural equations.

From the previous claim under the context $\boldsymbol{u}$ we have $V_c^0 = f_0(c)$ for all c. Therefore $(M_{\mathrm{unf}}(n, \Pi), \boldsymbol{u}) \models X{=}x$ by the definition of X and x. Similarly, for all $c \in C_E$ we have $V_c^n = f_n(c)$, so $(M_{\mathrm{unf}}(n, \Pi), \boldsymbol{u}) \models \varphi_E^n$. Hence $(M_{\mathrm{unf}}(n, \Pi), \boldsymbol{u}) \models (X{=}x) \wedge \varphi_E^n$, establishing HP-**AC1**.

By Definition 14 (**AC2^m**), there exist a witness set $W \subseteq \mathcal{C}$, an admissible interface-cut $\lambda = (C_1, I, C_2)$, and an intervention label $\theta \in \Theta$, such that, in our logic, $(\widehat{\mathcal{M}}, f_0, \Pi) \models \langle\theta\rangle(\chi_W(f_0) *_\lambda \delta_{C^* \setminus W}(f_0))$ and $(\widehat{\mathcal{M}}, f_0, \Pi) \models \langle\theta\rangle\square^+\neg\psi_E$. Informally, the first conjunct ensures that after θ there is a post-intervention configuration in which the witnesses W have their f_0-values while at least one coordinate in $C^\star \setminus W$ differs from its f_0-value; the second conjunct ensures that along all post-intervention continuations the effect ψ_E never holds.

We now translate this into the unfolded SCM. Define the set of time-0 variables $W' := \{ V_c^0 \mid c \in W \} \subseteq V$, and let $w^\star$ be the tuple of values $w^\star := (f_0(c))_{c \in W}$, viewed as an assignment to the variables in W'. Under the context $\boldsymbol{u}$, the equality $V_c^0 = f_0(c)$ holds for all c by the previous claim which we proved by induction. Therefore the logical condition $\chi_W(f_0)$ at time 0 corresponds exactly to the SCM assignment $[W' \leftarrow w^\star]$: it asserts that the variables in W' take their f_0-values.

The intervention θ is interpreted in the system semantics as $(\widehat{\mathcal{M}}, \Pi) \mapsto (\widehat{\mathcal{M}}_\theta, \Pi_\theta)$, and in the unfolding as a modified model $M_{\mathrm{unf}}^\theta(n, \Pi)$ in which, for each $c \in S_\theta$ and each $i \geq 1$, the right-hand side of the equation for V_c^i is replaced by the post-intervention mechanism $\mathcal{I}_c^{\Pi_\theta}$. This mirrors the mechanism-change semantics in the system model.

Consider now any assignment x' to X that differs from x on at least one coordinate corresponding to $C^\star \setminus W$. We define an initial configuration f_0' in the post-intervention system $(\widehat{\mathcal{M}}_\theta, \Pi_\theta)$ by

$$
f_0'(c) = \begin{cases}
f_0(c) & \text{if } c \in W, \\
x_c' & \text{if } c \in C^\star \setminus W, \\
f_0(c) & \text{if } c \notin C^\star,
\end{cases}
$$

where x_c' denotes the component of x' corresponding to V_c^0. By construction, f_0' satisfies $\chi_W(f_0)$ (the witnesses in W match f_0) and $\delta_{C^\star \setminus W}(f_0)$ (the values on $C^\star \setminus W$ differ from f_0 at least somewhere).

Let $(f_0', \ldots, f_n')$ be the (deterministic) run obtained in $(\widehat{\mathcal{M}}_\theta, \Pi_\theta)$ by starting from f_0' and applying the same schedule $(s_1, \ldots, s_n)$; the existence and uniqueness of such a run follow from the transition semantics and the fact that each step updates exactly one component using the corresponding mechanism in force. By repeating the unfolding construction with the modified mechanisms, we obtain the unfolded SCM $M_{\mathrm{unf}}^\theta(n, \Pi)$ and a context $\boldsymbol{u}' = (U_0 = f_0', S^i = s_i)$ whose unique solution satisfies $V_c^i = f_i'(c)$ for all $c \in C$ and $i = 0, \ldots, n$ in $M_{\mathrm{unf}}^\theta(n, \Pi)$, by the same induction argument as before.

By Definition 14($\mathbf{AC2}^m$), starting from f_0 and applying θ yields a post-intervention configuration with the W- and $C^\star \setminus W$-pattern of f_0'; moreover, along all post-intervention continuations from such a configuration, the effect ψ_E never holds. In particular, the outcome f_n' of the scheduled run starting at f_0' does not satisfy ψ_E. Under the unfolding, this means that the assignment to the variables $\{ V_c^n \mid c \in C_E \}$ in $M_{\mathrm{unf}}^\theta(n, \Pi)$ under $(\boldsymbol{u}', X \leftarrow x', W' \leftarrow w^\star)$ does *not* make φ_E^n true.

Finally, note that the intervention $[X \leftarrow x', W' \leftarrow w^\star]$ in $M_{\mathrm{unf}}^\theta(n, \Pi)$ plays exactly the role of fixing the time-0 variables corresponding to $C^\star$ and W to the values of f_0'; under $\boldsymbol{u}$, this yields the same solution as under $\boldsymbol{u}'$ because the structural equations for V_c^0 are determined entirely by U_0 and the interventions on X and W'. Thus we obtain $(M^\theta_{\mathrm{unf}}(n, \Pi), \boldsymbol{u}) \models [X \leftarrow x', W' \leftarrow w^*]\neg\varphi^n_E$, establishing HP-**AC2**.

Assume, for contradiction, that there exists a proper subset $X' \subset X$ that also satisfies HP-**AC1**–**AC2** as an actual cause of φ^n_E in $M_{\mathrm{unf}}(n, \Pi)$ under the same context $\boldsymbol{u}$. Let $C' \subsetneq C^\star$ be the corresponding subset of components, i.e. $X' = \{V^0_c \mid c \in C'\}$. By HP-**AC1** for X', we have $(M_{\mathrm{unf}}(n, \Pi), \boldsymbol{u}) \models X'{=}x' \wedge \varphi^n_E$ for some x', with x' agreeing with x on all components in C' (since the actual world is the same). By HP-**AC2** for X', there exist a (possibly empty) witness set $W'' \subseteq V$ and an assignment w'' and an alternative setting x'' on X' such that, in an appropriate modified unfolded model (corresponding to some mechanism-change intervention θ'), $(M^{\theta'}_{\mathrm{unf}}(n, \Pi), \boldsymbol{u}) \models [X' \leftarrow x'', W'' \leftarrow w'']\neg\varphi^n_E$.

By the same unfolding/collapse correspondence as in Step 2, this HP-**AC2** witness (X', x'', W'', w'') for $M^{\theta'}_{\mathrm{unf}}(n, \Pi)$ induces a corresponding triple (C', W', θ') in the system model that satisfies Definition 14(**AC2**^{m}) for C': we read W'' as a set of time-0 variables V^0_c, extract the underlying component set $W \subseteq C'$ from it, and use the same mechanism-change label θ'. HP-**AC1** guarantees that ψ_E holds at f_n and that C' has the appropriate actual values at f_0; HP-**AC2** guarantees that, under θ', an appropriate change to C' while holding W fixed prevents ψ_E along all post-intervention continuations. Thus C' satisfies Definition 14(**AC1**–**AC2**^{m}).

This contradicts the minimality clause (**AC3**) in Definition 14, which states that no proper subset of $C^\star$ can satisfy **AC1**–**AC2**^{m}. Hence no proper subset $X' \subset X$ can satisfy HP-**AC1**–**AC2**, and X is minimal in the HP sense.

We have shown that $X{=}x$ satisfies HP-**AC1**, HP-**AC2**, and HP-**AC3** as an actual cause of φ^n_E in $M_{\mathrm{unf}}(n, \Pi)$ under the context $\boldsymbol{u}$. This completes the proof. $\square$

In acyclic one-step dependency graphs, the time-unfolded SCM can be collapsed to a non-time-indexed SCM whose equations mirror the local mechanisms $\mathcal{I}^\Pi_c$. Our alignment result then specializes to the usual HP setting for such static models.

Remark 5. The use of $M^\theta_{\mathrm{unf}}(n, \Pi)$ in **AC2** corresponds to Halpern-Pearl's practice of taking counterfactuals with respect to a *modified model* when mechanisms are changed. For policy-labelled θ, the modification is exactly the replacement $\mathcal{I}^\Pi \to \mathcal{I}^{\Pi_\theta}$; for purely mechanistic θ, it rewrites the affected $\mathcal{I}_c$ in the equations.

For a simple illustration, consider a two-component system with components c_1, c_2 and influence context $\mathsf{Inf}(c_2) = \{c_1\}$. In the unfolded SCM for a one-step run, let $X := V^0_{c_1}$ and $Y := V^1_{c_2}$. The structural equations include an edge $X \to Y$ encoding the dependency of c_2 on c_1. Our alignment theorem then guarantees that any HP judgement about $X{=}x$ being an actual cause of a property of Y coincides with the corresponding causality judgement in the system model. $\square$

6   Application: LLM-RAG Workflows

Retrieval-augmented generation (RAG) couples a *retriever* that, given a query q, returns a small set of evidence items, with a *generator*, a Large Language Model

(LLM), that produces the final text conditioned on a context assembled from those items [18,31]. The architectural specifics (whether retrieval, re-ranking, or tools are neural, neuro-symbolic, or heuristic) do not matter here: our framework is implementation-agnostic. Operationally, retrieval and re-ranking produce a *context* that is handed off to the generator. The generator reads this context and emits a draft which is then filtered by a guard module. Tools may be invoked and their effects folded back into the context. Policies over these modules are supplied by *agents* (for example, an orchestrator for retrieval, re-ranking, and tool calls). This picture aligns with DSPy, a declarative framework that compiles structured modules into effective prompts and weights across base models, inference schemes, and learning algorithms [27].

In this view, LLM workflows are *text transformation graphs*: imperative computational graphs where LLMs are invoked through declarative, parametrized modules [27]. Our formal treatment complements this systematic development by giving a semantics for mechanism and policy edits, and connects these to Halpern-Pearl style causal claims. There is longstanding Information Retrieval work using counterfactual reasoning for evaluation and learning-to-rank [26], and recent strands inject explicit causal structure into retrieval and conditioning [39].

In parallel, a growing line connects formal verification with Halpern-Pearl actual causation to explain why properties hold or fail and to attribute responsibility within system models [6]. We lift this perspective to modular RAG workflows by making *interfaces* and *mechanism edits* first-class. This aligns with emerging assurance guidance: the NIST AI Risk Management Framework emphasizes lifecycle validation across context and outputs [33]; the UK Financial Conduct Authority advocates technology-agnostic oversight oriented to firms' systems and processes [16]. Cloud-operations guidance such as AWS's MLOps white-paper treats reliability and governance as end-to-end workflow properties with auditable, reproducible edits and controls [2].

In particular, we model a (stylized) RAG software-workflow (with tools and guards) as an augmented system $\widehat{\mathcal{M}} = (\mathcal{C}, \mathcal{B}, \mathcal{I}, F, \Delta_{\mathcal{I}}, \Gamma, \mathsf{cut}, [\![\cdot]\!])$ with agents as in Sect. 3. The goal is to reason modularly about edits to mechanisms and policies while preserving invariants across named interfaces. In particular, inputs/outputs are not components in our framework, but are represented as *behaviours of interface components*. Thus the context passed from retrieval to generation is the behaviour of a dedicated component CtxOut, and decoder requests to tools are behaviours of Dec.

The component set is $\mathcal{C} = \{$Tok, Retr, Rank, CtxOut, Dec, Guard, Tool, Mem, PortCtx, PortDecReq$\}$:

1. Tok (*tokenizer*): parses the user input into tokens, and is the source of retrieval queries.
2. Retr (*retriever*): fetches candidate documents given Tok (and possibly Mem).
3. Rank (*ranker/re-ranker*): orders Retr's candidates.
4. CtxOut (*context builder*): composes the prompt(context) from Rank (and Mem) for the LLM instance.

5. Dec (*decoder*): produces model outputs conditioned on the interface context and tool state.
6. Guard (*guardrail*): vets drafts produced by Dec and either blocks or permits responses.
7. Tool (*tool executor*): executes external tool calls (search, code, database connector, etc.).
8. Mem (*memory cache*): stores and retrieves auxiliary state (e.g., past interactions, embeddings) influencing Retr and observed by Dec.
9. PortCtx (*context port*): It holds the hand-off value written by a designated intervention (e.g., $\theta_{\mathrm{pushCtx}}$) summarizing CtxOut. It is influenced by no other component.
10. PortDecReq (*tool-request port*): This component is toggled by a designated intervention (e.g., $\theta_{\mathrm{callTool}}$) to signal tool invocation. It is influenced by no other component.

The Model Context Protocol (MCP) [4] is an open standard that lets instances of LLM agents connect in a standardized, two-way, client-server way to external tools and data sources enabling them to discover and to invoke external tools and pull context. In practice, CtxOut, PortCtx, and PortDecReq correspond directly to the hand-off points defined by MCP. CtxOut implements client-side assembly from MCP prompts, writing PortCtx is the commit of the constructed model input to the decoder, and toggling PortDecReq mirrors MCP tool invocations. We model each component with only finitely many behaviours, and dependencies are expressed through influence contexts:

$$\mathbb{B}(\mathsf{Tok}) = \{\mathsf{ok}, \mathsf{err}\} \qquad \mathbb{B}(\mathsf{Retr}) = \{\mathsf{none}, \mathsf{rel}, \mathsf{spur}\}$$
$$\mathbb{B}(\mathsf{Rank}) = \{\mathsf{good}, \mathsf{bad}\} \qquad \mathbb{B}(\mathsf{CtxOut}) = \{\mathsf{short}, \mathsf{long}, \mathsf{noctx}\}$$
$$\mathbb{B}(\mathsf{Dec}) = \{\mathsf{safe}, \mathsf{unsafe}, \mathsf{abort}\} \qquad \mathbb{B}(\mathsf{Guard}) = \{\mathsf{pass}, \mathsf{block}\}$$
$$\mathbb{B}(\mathsf{Tool}) = \{\mathsf{off}, \mathsf{on}, \mathsf{fail}\} \qquad \mathbb{B}(\mathsf{Mem}) = \{\mathsf{hit}, \mathsf{miss}\}$$
$$\mathbb{B}(\mathsf{PortCtx}) = \{\mathsf{short}, \mathsf{long}, \mathsf{noctx}\} \qquad \mathbb{B}(\mathsf{PortDecReq}) = \{\mathsf{off}, \mathsf{on}\}$$

$$\mathsf{Inf}(\mathsf{Tok}) = \varnothing \qquad \mathsf{Inf}(\mathsf{Retr}) = \{\mathsf{Tok}, \mathsf{Mem}\} \qquad \mathsf{Inf}(\mathsf{Rank}) = \{\mathsf{Retr}\}$$
$$\mathsf{Inf}(\mathsf{CtxOut}) = \{\mathsf{Rank}, \mathsf{Mem}\} \qquad \mathsf{Inf}(\mathsf{PortCtx}) = \varnothing \qquad \mathsf{Inf}(\mathsf{Dec}) = \{\mathsf{PortCtx}\}$$
$$\mathsf{Inf}(\mathsf{Guard}) = \{\mathsf{Dec}\} \qquad \mathsf{Inf}(\mathsf{PortDecReq}) = \varnothing$$
$$\mathsf{Inf}(\mathsf{Mem}) = \{\mathsf{Retr}\} \qquad \mathsf{Inf}(\mathsf{Tool}) = \{\mathsf{PortDecReq}\}$$

We set $\mathsf{Inf}(\mathsf{Tok}) = \varnothing$ because Tok is the RAG workflow's exogenous source: it updates from user input, not from any modelled component. Let $\mathcal{A} = \{\mathsf{Orch}, \mathsf{Safety}\}$ be a set denoting agents: orchestrator and safety owner. A relation $\mathrm{Ctrl} \subseteq \mathcal{A} \times \mathcal{C}$ with $\mathrm{Ctrl}(\mathsf{Orch}) = \{\mathsf{Retr}, \mathsf{Rank}, \mathsf{CtxOut}, \mathsf{Dec}, \mathsf{Tool}\}$ and $\mathrm{Ctrl}(\mathsf{Safety}) = \{\mathsf{Guard}\}$ specifies which agent controls which components. A policy profile $\Pi = (\pi_{\mathsf{Orch}}, \pi_{\mathsf{Safety}})$ parametrizes the local rules (cf. Sect. 3). Thus each component c consumes only $(f(d))_{d \in \mathsf{Inf}(c)}$ (e.g., Dec sees only PortCtx; Tool sees only PortDecReq). We use interventions $\theta[\mathsf{PortCtx}]$ and $\theta[\mathsf{PortDecReq}]$ for port writes. We use two admissible interface cuts $(C_1^{\mathrm{retr}}, I^{\mathrm{retr}}, C_2^{\mathrm{gen}})$ and

$(C_1^{\text{tool}}, I^{\text{tool}}, C_2^{\text{rest}})$ (cf. Definition 6) with

$$
\begin{aligned}
I^{\text{tool}} &= \{\mathsf{PortDecReq}\} & C_1^{\text{retr}} &= \{\mathsf{Tok}, \mathsf{Retr}, \mathsf{Rank}, \mathsf{Mem}, \mathsf{CtxOut}, \mathsf{PortCtx}\} \\
I^{\text{retr}} &= \{\mathsf{PortCtx}\} & C_2^{\text{gen}} &= \{\mathsf{PortCtx}, \mathsf{Dec}, \mathsf{Guard}, \mathsf{Tool}, \mathsf{PortDecReq}\} \\
C_1^{\text{tool}} &= \{\mathsf{Tool}, \mathsf{PortDecReq}\} & C_2^{\text{rest}} &= \{\mathsf{Tok}, \mathsf{Retr}, \mathsf{Rank}, \mathsf{Mem}, \mathsf{CtxOut}, \mathsf{PortCtx}, \\
& & & \qquad \mathsf{PortDecReq}, \mathsf{Dec}, \mathsf{Guard}\}
\end{aligned}
$$

Admissibility holds since $\mathsf{Inf}(c) \subseteq C_1^{\text{retr}} \cup I^{\text{retr}}$ for $c \in C_1^{\text{retr}} \setminus I^{\text{retr}}$, and similarly for C_2^{gen}. Similarly, $\mathsf{Inf}(c) \subseteq C_1^{\text{tool}} \cup I^{\text{tool}}$ for $c \in C_1^{\text{tool}} \setminus I^{\text{tool}}$, and likewise for C_2^{rest}. Also, $\mathsf{Inf}(\mathsf{PortCtx}) = \varnothing \subseteq I^{\text{retr}}$.

Representative Queries. Atomic propositions are of the form $p_{X=\sigma}$ ('X exhibits behaviour σ'). Let $\mathsf{bad} \equiv (p_{\mathsf{Dec=unsafe}} \wedge p_{\mathsf{Guard=pass}})$.

1. **Guarded recovery.** Assume the policy-labelled edit $\theta_{\mathsf{policySaf}}$ rewrites only Guard and enforces $\mathcal{I}_{\mathsf{Guard}}^{\theta_{\mathsf{policySaf}}}(f) = \mathsf{block}$ whenever $f(\mathsf{Dec}) = \mathsf{unsafe}$. Then we have $(\widehat{\mathcal{M}}, f, \Pi) \models \langle \theta_{\mathsf{policySaf}} \rangle \square \neg \mathsf{bad}$. Moreover, if the schedule re-evaluates Guard on every step that can change Dec, then the guarantee strengthens to $(\widehat{\mathcal{M}}, f, \Pi) \models \langle \theta_{\mathsf{policySaf}} \rangle \square^{+} \neg \mathsf{bad}$.

2. Let $\lambda = \lambda_{\text{retr-gen}}$ with interface $\mathsf{PortCtx}$ and write φ_{C_1} for any C_1-local property over $\{\mathsf{Tok}, \mathsf{Retr}, \mathsf{Rank}, \mathsf{Mem}, \mathsf{CtxOut}, \mathsf{PortCtx}\}$ and ψ_{C_2} for any C_2-local property over $\{\mathsf{Dec}, \mathsf{Guard}, \mathsf{Tool}, \mathsf{PortDecReq}\}$. If θ rewrites only Retr (hence only C_1) and preserves the cut, then $((\widehat{\mathcal{M}}, f, \Pi) \models \varphi_{C_1} *_\lambda \psi_{C_2}) \to ((\widehat{\mathcal{M}}, f, \Pi) \models \langle \theta \rangle (\varphi_{C_1} *_\lambda \Diamond^{+} \psi_{C_2}))$. In particular, C_1-facts are preserved and C_2-facts can be re-established after applying θ.

3. **Actual-cause.** Let $f \rightsquigarrow f'$ denote a non-empty path (one or more steps) under the current policy profile Π. Let the effect be $\psi_E := p_{\mathsf{Dec=unsafe}} \wedge p_{\mathsf{Guard=pass}}$ (decoder unsafe and guard passes at f'). We test $C^{\star} = \{\mathsf{Retr}, \mathsf{Rank}\}$ as the candidate cause-set and use $W = \{\mathsf{PortCtx}\}$ as the witness held fixed at the retrieval-generation interface $\lambda_{\text{retr-gen}}$. ψ_E holds at f' and the components in $C^{\star}$ are unchanged along $f \rightsquigarrow f'$. For an admissible intervention θ that alters some element of $C^{\star} \setminus W$ (e.g. $\theta_{\mathsf{top\text{-}k}(k)}$ or $\theta_{\mathsf{tok\text{-}swap}}$) while $\lambda_{\text{retr-gen}}$ is preserved, we require $(\widehat{\mathcal{M}}, f, \Pi) \models \langle \theta \rangle (\chi_W(f) *_{\lambda_{\text{retr-gen}}} \delta_{C^{\star} \setminus W}(f))$ and $(\widehat{\mathcal{M}}, f, \Pi) \models \langle \theta \rangle \square^{+} \neg (\psi_E \wedge \chi_{C^{\star}}(f))$. No proper subset of $C^{\star}$ satisfies these conditions.

7 Metatheory: Soundness and Completeness

We now state and prove our main metatheoretic results. Under mild finiteness conditions (Definition 15), logical equivalence in $\mathcal{L}(\langle \theta \rangle, *_\Lambda)$ implies a cut-preserving bisimulation under intervention (cf. [5,8]).

Definition 15. *An augmented model $\widehat{\mathcal{M}}$ is image-finite if every $f \in F$ has finitely many $\Delta_{\mathcal{I}}$-successors. We say the label sets Θ and Λ are operationally finite for $\widehat{\mathcal{M}}$ if only finitely many interventions $\theta \in \Theta$ have $\widehat{\mathcal{M}}_\theta$ well-defined and pairwise distinct, and only finitely many $\lambda \in \Lambda$ are admissible in $\widehat{\mathcal{M}}$.* $\qquad \square$

Definition 16 (Bisimulation under intervention and cuts). *Let $\widehat{\mathcal{M}}_i$ be interface-admitting augmented models with configuration sets F_i and policy profiles Π_i $(i = 1, 2)$. A relation $\mathscr{R}$ between pointed system models $(\widehat{\mathcal{M}}_1, f_1, \Pi_1)$ and $(\widehat{\mathcal{M}}_2, f_2, \Pi_2)$ is a* cut-preserving bisimulation under intervention *if the following hold whenever $(\widehat{\mathcal{M}}_1, f_1, \Pi_1)\,\mathscr{R}\,(\widehat{\mathcal{M}}_2, f_2, \Pi_2)$:*

1. *$\textbf{Atoms.}$ For all atoms $p \in \mathcal{P}$, $(\widehat{\mathcal{M}}_1, f_1, \Pi_1) \models p$ iff $(\widehat{\mathcal{M}}_2, f_2, \Pi_2) \models p$.*
2. *$\textbf{Steps (forth/back).}$ If $f_1 \Delta_{\mathcal{I}_1}^{\Pi_1} y_1$, then there exists $y_2 \in F_2$ such that $f_2 \Delta_{\mathcal{I}_2}^{\Pi_2} y_2$ and $(\widehat{\mathcal{M}}_1, y_1, \Pi_1)\,\mathscr{R}\,(\widehat{\mathcal{M}}_2, y_2, \Pi_2)$. Symmetrically for steps from f_2.*
3. *$\textbf{Interventions.}$ For every $\theta \in \Theta$, write $[\![\theta]\!](\widehat{\mathcal{M}}_i, \Pi_i) = (\widehat{\mathcal{M}}_{i,\theta}, \Pi_{i,\theta})$ and let $\Delta_{\mathcal{I}_{i,\theta}}^{\Pi_{i,\theta}}$ be the induced transition relation in $\widehat{\mathcal{M}}_{i,\theta}$. If there exists y_1 with $f_1(\Delta_{\mathcal{I}_{1,\theta}}^{\Pi_{1,\theta}})^\star y_1$ in $\widehat{\mathcal{M}}_{1,\theta}$, then there exists y_2 with $f_2(\Delta_{\mathcal{I}_{2,\theta}}^{\Pi_{2,\theta}})^\star y_2$ in $\widehat{\mathcal{M}}_{2,\theta}$ and $(\widehat{\mathcal{M}}_{1,\theta}, y_1, \Pi_{1,\theta})\mathscr{R}(\widehat{\mathcal{M}}_{2,\theta}, y_2, \Pi_{2,\theta})$. The symmetric condition holds starting from f_2.*
4. *$\textbf{Indexed separation.}$ If $\lambda \in \Lambda$ is admissible at $(\widehat{\mathcal{M}}_1, f_1, \Pi_1)$ with $\mathsf{cut}_1(\lambda) = (C_1^1, I^1, C_2^1)$, then there exists $\lambda' \in \Lambda$ admissible at the second pointed system model $(\widehat{\mathcal{M}}_2, f_2, \Pi_2)$ with $\mathsf{cut}_2(\lambda') = (C_1^2, I^2, C_2^2)$ such that, for $j = 1, 2$, $(\widehat{\mathcal{M}}_1\!\restriction_{C_j^1}, f_1 \restriction_{C_j^1}, \Pi_1)\,\mathscr{R}\,(\widehat{\mathcal{M}}_2\!\restriction_{C_j^2}, f_2 \restriction_{C_j^2}, \Pi_2)$. The symmetric condition holds exchanging 1 and 2.*

□

Remark 6. A relation that satisfies items *(1)–(3)* of Definition 16 is called an *intervention-preserving bisimulation*. A *cut-preserving* bisimulation under intervention additionally satisfies item *(4)* for the indexed separating connective.   □

Theorem 2 (Completeness / Hennessy–Milner property). *Let $(\widehat{\mathcal{M}}_1, f_1, \Pi_1)$ and $(\widehat{\mathcal{M}}_2, f_2, \Pi_2)$ be interface-admitting, image-finite pointed models whose label sets Θ, Λ are operationally finite. Assume that for all $\varphi \in \mathcal{L}(\langle\theta\rangle, *_\Lambda)$,*

$$(\widehat{\mathcal{M}}_1, f_1, \Pi_1) \models \varphi \text{ iff } (\widehat{\mathcal{M}}_2, f_2, \Pi_2) \models \varphi.$$

Then there exists a relation $\mathscr{R}$ such that $(\widehat{\mathcal{M}}_1, f_1, \Pi_1)\,\mathscr{R}\,(\widehat{\mathcal{M}}_2, f_2, \Pi_2)$ and $\mathscr{R}$ is a cut-preserving bisimulation under intervention.   □

Proof. For any pointed model $x = (\widehat{\mathcal{M}}, f, \Pi)$ write $\mathsf{Th}(x) := \{\varphi \in \mathcal{L}(\langle\theta\rangle, *_\Lambda) \mid x \models \varphi\}$. Define $\mathscr{R} := \{(x_1, x_2) \mid \mathsf{Th}(x_1) = \mathsf{Th}(x_2)\}$. We show that $\mathscr{R}$ satisfies the clauses of Definition 16.

Atoms. Immediate from $\mathsf{Th}(x_1) = \mathsf{Th}(x_2)$.

Steps (forth/back). Fix $(\widehat{\mathcal{M}}_1, f_1, \Pi_1)\,\mathscr{R}\,(\widehat{\mathcal{M}}_2, f_2, \Pi_2)$. By image-finiteness the successor sets $\mathrm{Succ}_i(f_i) := \{g \mid f_i \Delta_{\mathcal{I}_i}^{\Pi_i} g\}$ are finite. By a standard Hennessy-Milner argument, there exists a finite *characteristic family* $\{\chi_j^1\}_{j \in J}$ of formulae such that each $g \in \mathrm{Succ}_1(f_1)$ satisfies exactly one χ_j^1, and distinct successors satisfy distinct χ_j^1. Then

$$(\widehat{\mathcal{M}}_1, f_1, \Pi_1) \models \Diamond\Big(\bigvee_{j \in J} \chi_j^1\Big) \quad \text{iff} \quad (\widehat{\mathcal{M}}_2, f_2, \Pi_2) \models \Diamond\Big(\bigvee_{j \in J} \chi_j^1\Big),$$

so there exists g_2 with $f_2 \, \Delta_{\mathcal{I}_2}^{\Pi_2} \, g_2$ and $(\widehat{\mathcal{M}}_2, g_2, \Pi_2) \models \chi_{j^*}^1$ for some $j^* \in J$. By construction, there is $g_1 \in \mathrm{Succ}_1(f_1)$ with $(\widehat{\mathcal{M}}_1, g_1, \Pi_1) \models \chi_{j^*}^1$, and hence $\mathrm{Th}(\widehat{\mathcal{M}}_1, g_1, \Pi_1) = \mathrm{Th}(\widehat{\mathcal{M}}_2, g_2, \Pi_2)$. Thus $(\widehat{\mathcal{M}}_1, g_1, \Pi_1) \, \mathscr{R} \, (\widehat{\mathcal{M}}_2, g_2, \Pi_2)$. The back direction is symmetric.

Interventions. Fix $\theta \in \Theta$. Write $[\![\theta]\!](\widehat{\mathcal{M}}_i, \Pi_i) = (\widehat{\mathcal{M}}_{i,\theta}, \Pi_{i,\theta})$ and let

$$R_i(\theta) := \big\{ \, g \; \big| \; f_i \, (\Delta_{\mathcal{I}_{i,\theta}}^{\Pi_{i,\theta}})^\star \, g \text{ in } \widehat{\mathcal{M}}_{i,\theta} \, \big\}.$$

By operational finiteness of Θ and image-finiteness, each $R_i(\theta)$ is finite. Again by a Hennessy–Milner argument, there exists a finite characteristic family $\{\psi_k^1\}_{k \in K}$ for $R_1(\theta)$ in $\mathcal{L}(\langle\theta\rangle, *_\Lambda)$. If $(\widehat{\mathcal{M}}_1, f_1, \Pi_1) \models \langle\theta\rangle\psi_k^1$, then $\langle\theta\rangle\psi_k^1 \in \mathrm{Th}(\widehat{\mathcal{M}}_1, f_1, \Pi_1) = \mathrm{Th}(\widehat{\mathcal{M}}_2, f_2, \Pi_2)$, so $(\widehat{\mathcal{M}}_2, f_2, \Pi_2) \models \langle\theta\rangle\psi_k^1$. Hence there exists $g_2 \in R_2(\theta)$ with $(\widehat{\mathcal{M}}_{2,\theta}, g_2, \Pi_{2,\theta}) \models \psi_k^1$. By characteristic completeness, there is $g_1 \in R_1(\theta)$ with $(\widehat{\mathcal{M}}_{1,\theta}, g_1, \Pi_{1,\theta}) \models \psi_k^1$ and $\mathrm{Th}(\widehat{\mathcal{M}}_{1,\theta}, g_1, \Pi_{1,\theta}) = \mathrm{Th}(\widehat{\mathcal{M}}_{2,\theta}, g_2, \Pi_{2,\theta})$, so $(\widehat{\mathcal{M}}_{1,\theta}, g_1, \Pi_{1,\theta}) \, \mathscr{R} \, (\widehat{\mathcal{M}}_{2,\theta}, g_2, \Pi_{2,\theta})$. The back direction is symmetric.

Indexed separation. By operational finiteness of Λ, at each pointed state only finitely many cut labels are admissible. Suppose λ is admissible at $(\widehat{\mathcal{M}}_1, f_1, \Pi_1)$ with $\mathrm{cut}_1(\lambda) = (C_1^1, I^1, C_2^1)$. Let $\{\alpha_p\}$ be a finite characteristic family for $(\widehat{\mathcal{M}}_1 {\restriction} C_1^1, f_1 {\restriction} C_1^1, \Pi_1)$ and $\{\beta_q\}$ a finite characteristic family for $(\widehat{\mathcal{M}}_1 {\restriction} C_2^1, f_1 {\restriction} C_2^1, \Pi_1)$. Consider the finite set of formulae $\mathcal{S}_\lambda := \{ \, \alpha_p *_\lambda \beta_q \mid p, q \, \}$. For every $\sigma \in \mathcal{S}_\lambda$ we have $\sigma \in \mathrm{Th}(\widehat{\mathcal{M}}_1, f_1, \Pi_1)$ iff $\sigma \in \mathrm{Th}(\widehat{\mathcal{M}}_2, f_2, \Pi_2)$. It follows that there exists some admissible cut $\lambda' = (C_1^2, I^2, C_2^2)$ at $(\widehat{\mathcal{M}}_2, f_2, \Pi_2)$ such that the same pattern of α_p / β_q-truth is witnessed in the corresponding restricted models. From the characteristic property of the families, we conclude that, for $j = 1, 2$, $(\widehat{\mathcal{M}}_1 {\restriction} C_j^1, f_1 {\restriction} C_j^1, \Pi_1) \, \mathscr{R} \, (\widehat{\mathcal{M}}_2 {\restriction} C_j^2, f_2 {\restriction} C_j^2, \Pi_2)$. The symmetric argument starting from a cut at $(\widehat{\mathcal{M}}_2, f_2, \Pi_2)$ yields the back condition. Thus $\mathscr{R}$ is a cut-preserving bisimulation under intervention relating $(\widehat{\mathcal{M}}_1, f_1, \Pi_1)$ and $(\widehat{\mathcal{M}}_2, f_2, \Pi_2)$. $\square$

Soundness is established for the *restricted* language $\mathcal{L}(\langle\theta\rangle)$ without the indexed separating connective $*_\lambda$ (cf. [3], which solves a similar problem).

Theorem 3 (Soundness).   *If two image-finite pointed models $(\widehat{\mathcal{M}}_1, f_1, \Pi_1)$ and $(\widehat{\mathcal{M}}_2, f_2, \Pi_2)$ are intervention-preserving bisimilar, then, for all $\varphi \in \mathcal{L}(\langle\theta\rangle)$,*

$$(\widehat{\mathcal{M}}_1, f_1, \Pi_1) \models \varphi \quad \text{iff} \quad (\widehat{\mathcal{M}}_2, f_2, \Pi_2) \models \varphi.$$

$\square$

Proof. By structural induction on φ.

1. *Atoms and Boolean connectives:* Immediate from the atoms clause of the bisimulation and the induction hypothesis.
2. Suppose $(\widehat{\mathcal{M}}_1, f_1, \Pi_1) \models \Diamond\psi$. Then there exists f_1' with $f_1 \Delta_{\mathcal{I}_1}^{\Pi_1} f_1'$, and it holds that $(\widehat{\mathcal{M}}_1, f_1', \Pi_1) \models \psi$. By the step-*forth* clause, there exists f_2' with $f_2 \Delta_{\mathcal{I}_2}^{\Pi_2} f_2'$ and $(\widehat{\mathcal{M}}_1, f_1', \Pi_1)\mathscr{R}(\widehat{\mathcal{M}}_2, f_2', \Pi_2)$. By the induction hypothesis, we have $(\widehat{\mathcal{M}}_2, f_2', \Pi_2) \models \psi$, hence $(\widehat{\mathcal{M}}_2, f_2, \Pi_2) \models \Diamond\psi$. The converse uses the step-*back* clause, and the $\Box$-case is analogous.
3. Suppose $(\widehat{\mathcal{M}}_1, f_1, \Pi_1) \models \langle\theta\rangle\psi$. By the semantics of $\langle\theta\rangle$ there exists f_1' such that $[\![\theta]\!](\widehat{\mathcal{M}}_1, \Pi_1) = (\widehat{\mathcal{M}}_{1,\theta}, \Pi_{1,\theta})$, $f_1(\Delta_{\mathcal{I}_{1,\theta}}^{\Pi_{1,\theta}})^\star f_1'$, and $(\widehat{\mathcal{M}}_{1,\theta}, f_1', \Pi_{1,\theta}) \models \psi$. By the intervention clause of the bisimulation relation, there exists f_2' such that $[\![\theta]\!](\widehat{\mathcal{M}}_2, \Pi_2) = (\widehat{\mathcal{M}}_{2,\theta}, \Pi_{2,\theta})$, $f_2(\Delta_{\mathcal{I}_{2,\theta}}^{\Pi_{2,\theta}})^\star f_2'$. Furthermore it follows that $(\widehat{\mathcal{M}}_{1,\theta}, f_1', \Pi_{1,\theta})\mathscr{R}(\widehat{\mathcal{M}}_{2,\theta}, f_2', \Pi_{2,\theta})$. By the induction hypothesis (applied inside the intervened models), $(\widehat{\mathcal{M}}_{2,\theta}, f_2', \Pi_{2,\theta}) \models \psi$. Therefore $(\widehat{\mathcal{M}}_2, f_2, \Pi_2) \models \langle\theta\rangle\psi$. The converse implication is symmetric and uses the *back* direction of the intervention clause.

8   Conclusion

The language $\mathcal{L}(\langle\theta\rangle, *_\Lambda)$ combines a single intervention modality $\langle\theta\rangle$ with an *indexed* separating conjunction $*_\lambda$, enabling modular reasoning across interfaces. Agent policies are captured as interventions in the same language. We have defined actual causation directly in this logic and established alignment with the Halpern–Pearl account of actual causation via a time-unfolding construction. We have also established a soundness-and-completeness result in the form of a Hennessy–Milner–van Benthem–Bergstra bisimulation-invariance theorem under natural finiteness assumptions [7].

Our present account has two main limitations: we assume fixed interfaces, and our reasoning is qualitative. These constraints suggest concrete extensions. Drawing on quantitative model checking [12], we can place probabilities on system-configuration transitions. We can also enrich the logic with quantitative modalities so that optimisation claims such as "the minimum accumulated cost of changing mechanisms ensuring φ is c" become expressible, where costs range over budgets, compute quotas, and permission/approval requirements, in line with emerging governance standards [25]. Interfaces and influence contexts may be allowed to evolve, capturing how mechanisms and dependencies are re-learned or reconfigured as systems adapt; this connects to work on causal-structure learning and dynamic causal discovery [14,36].

Taken together, these extensions—all expressible within a single language for configuration transitions, interventions, and modular decompositions—point toward a unified, certifiable logic of causal design, supporting probabilistic guarantees, cost-aware mechanism change, and adaptive boundaries for evolving multiagent systems.

Acknowledgements. Chakraborty is supported by a studentship from UCL's EPSRC-funded Centre for Doctoral Training in Cybersecurity (EP/S022503/1).

References

1. Alur, R., Henzinger, T.A., Kupferman, O.: Alternating-time temporal logic. J. ACM **49**(5), 672–713 (2002). https://doi.org/10.1145/585265.585270
2. Amazon Web Services: MLOps: Continuous Delivery for Machine Learning on AWS (2020). https://d1.awsstatic.com/whitepapers/mlops-continuous-delivery-machine-learning-on-aws.pdf
3. Anderson, G., Pym, D.: A calculus and logic of bunched resources and processes. Theor. Comput. Sci. **614**(C), 63–96 (2016). https://doi.org/10.1016/j.tcs.2015.11.035
4. Anthropic: Model Context Protocol. https://modelcontextprotocol.io/specification/2025-06-18
5. Aucher, G., van Benthem, J., Grossi, D.: Modal logics of sabotage revisited. J. Log. Computat. **28**(2), 269–303 (2017). https://doi.org/10.1093/logcom/exx034
6. Baier, C., et al.: From verification to causality-based explications. In: LIPIcs 198: 48th Int. Colloq. Automata, Languages, and Programming (ICALP 2021), pp. 1:1–1:20 (2021). https://doi.org/10.4230/LIPIcs.ICALP.2021.1
7. van Benthem, J., Bergstra, J.: Logic of transition systems. J. Log. Lang. Inf. **3**(4), 247–283 (1994). https://doi.org/10.1007/bf01160018
8. Blackburn, P., de Rijke, M., Venema, Y.: Modal logic. CUP (2001)
9. Bujorianu, M., Caulfield, T., Ilau, M.C., Pym, D.: Interfaces in ecosystems: Concepts, form, and implement. In: Juan, A.A., Guisado-Lizar, JL., Morón-Fernández, MJ., Perez-Bernabeu, E. (eds) Simulation Tools and Techniques. SIMUtools 2024. LNICS. vol. 603, pp. 27–47. Springer, Cham (2025). https://doi.org/10.1007/978-3-031-87345-4_3
10. Caulfield, T., Ilau, M.-C., Pym, D.: Engineering ecosystem models: semantics and pragmatics. In: Jiang, D., Song, H. (eds.) SIMUtools 2021. LNICST, vol. 424, pp. 236–258. Springer, Cham (2022). https://doi.org/10.1007/978-3-030-97124-3_21
11. Chakraborty, P., Caulfield, T., Pym, D.: Causality and decision-making: a logical framework for systems and security modelling (2025). https://arxiv.org/abs/2508.01758
12. Chen, T., Forejt, V., Kwiatkowska, M., Parker, D., Simaitis, A.: Prism-games: a model checker for stochastic multi-player games. In: Proceedings of the 19th International Conference on Tools and Algorithms for the Construction and Analysis of Systems, pp. 185–191 (2013). https://doi.org/10.1007/978-3-642-36742-7_13
13. Dubslaff, C.e.a.: Causality in configurable software systems. In: Proceedings of the 44th International Conference on Software Engineering, pp. 325–337. Association for Computing Machinery (2022). https://doi.org/10.1145/3510003.3510200
14. Eberhardt, F.: Introduction to the epistemology of causation. Philos Compass **4**(6), 913–925 (2009). https://doi.org/10.1111/j.1747-9991.2009.00243.x
15. Everitt, T., Carey, R., Langlois, E.D., Ortega, P.A., Legg, S.: Agent incentives: a causal perspective. In: Proceedings of the AAAI Conference on Artificial Intelligence, **35**(13), pp. 11487–11495 (May 2021). https://doi.org/10.1609/aaai.v35i13.17368
16. Financial Conduct Authority, United Kingdom: Artificial Intelligence (AI) update (2024). https://www.fca.org.uk/publication/corporate/ai-update.pdf

17. Galmiche, D., Lang, T., Pym, D.: Minimalistic system modelling: behaviours, interfaces, and local reasoning. In: Juan, A.A., Guisado-Lizar, JL., Morón-Fernández, MJ., Perez-Bernabeu, E. (eds) Simulation Tools and Techniques. SIMUtools 2024. LNICS, SITE, vol. 603. Springer, Cham (2024). https://doi.org/10.48550/arXiv.2401.16109, https://doi.org/10.1007/978-3-031-87345-4_4. Accessed 9 Jun 2025

18. Gao, Y. et al.: Retrieval-augmented generation for large language models: a survey (2024). https://arxiv.org/abs/2312.10997

19. Geiger, A., Lu, H., Icard, T., Potts, C.: Causal abstractions of neural networks. In: Proc. 35th Int. Conf. on Neural Information Processing Systems (2021)

20. Gladyshev, M., Alechina, N., Dastani, M., Doder, D.: Dynamics of causal dependencies in multi-agent settings. In: Ciortea, A., Dastani, M., Luo, J. (eds) Engineering Multi-Agent Systems (EMAS 2023). LNCS, vol. 14378, pp. 95–112. Springer, Cham (2023). https://doi.org/10.1007/978-3-031-48539-8_7

21. Halpern, J.Y.: Actual Causality. The MIT Press (2016). https://doi.org/10.7551/mitpress/10809.001.0001

22. Halpern, J.Y., Pearl, J.: Causes and explanations: a structural-model approach. Part I: Causes. Brit. J. Phil. Sci. **56**(4), 843–887 (2005)

23. Hammond, L., Fox, J., Everitt, T., Carey, R., Abate, A., Wooldridge, M.: Reasoning about causality in games. Artif. Intell. **320**, 103919 (2023). https://doi.org/10.1016/j.artint.2023.103919

24. Howard, R.A., Matheson, J.E.: Influence diagrams. Decis. Anal. **2**(3), 127–143 (2005). https://doi.org/10.1287/deca.1050.0020

25. International Organization for Standardization: ISO/IEC 42001:2023 — information technology — artificial intelligence management systems. https://www.iso.org/standard/81230.html (2023)

26. Joachims, T., Swaminathan, A.: Counterfactual evaluation and learning for search, recommendation and ad placement. In: Proc. 39th Int. ACM SIGIR Conf. on Research and Development in Information Retrieval, pp. 1199–1201 (2016). https://doi.org/10.1145/2911451.2914803

27. Khattab, O. et al.: DSPy: Compiling Declarative Language Model Calls into Self-Improving Pipelines (2023). https://arxiv.org/abs/2310.03714

28. Koller, D., Friedman, N.: Probabilistic Graphical Models: Principles and Techniques. The MIT Press (2009)

29. Koller, D., Milch, B.: Multi-agent influence diagrams for representing and solving games. Games Econom. Behav. **45**(1), 181–221 (2003). https://doi.org/10.1016/S0899-8256(02)00544-4

30. Krishna, R., Iqbal, M.S., Javidian, M.A., Ray, B., Jamshidi, P.: CADET: Debugging and Fixing Misconfigurations using Counterfactual Reasoning (2021). https://arxiv.org/abs/2010.06061

31. Lewis, P., et al.: Retrieval-augmented generation for knowledge-intensive NLP tasks. In: Proc. 34th Int. Conf. on Neural Information Processing Systems (2020)

32. Machamer, P., Darden, L., Craver, C.F.: Thinking about mechanisms. Philos. Sci. **67**(1), 1–25 (2000). https://doi.org/10.1086/392759

33. National Institute of Standards and Technology, U.S. Department of Commerce: Artificial Intelligence Risk Management Framework (2024). https://nvlpubs.nist.gov/nistpubs/ai/nist.ai.100-1.pdf

34. O'Hearn, P.W., Pym, D.J.: The logic of bunched implications. Bull. Symbolic Logic **5**(2), 215–244 (1999). https://doi.org/10.2307/421090

35. Pearl, J.: Causality: Models, Reasoning and Inference. CUP, 2nd edn. (2009)

36. Schölkopf, B., Locatello, F., Bauer, S., Ke, N.R., Kalchbrenner, N., Goyal, A., Bengio, Y.: Toward Causal Representation Learning. Proc. IEEE **109**(5), 612–634 (2021)
37. Shachter, R.D.: Evaluating influence diagrams. Oper. Res. **34**(6), 871–882 (1986). https://doi.org/10.1287/opre.34.6.871
38. Simon, H.A., Barnard, C.I.: Administrative Behavior: A study of Decision-making Processes in Administrative Organization. Macmillan Co. (1947)
39. Wang, N., Han, X., Singh, J., Ma, J., Chaudhary, V.: CausalRAG: integrating causal graphs into retrieval-augmented generation. In: Findings of the Association for Computational Linguistics: ACL 2025, pp. 22680–22693 (2025). https://doi.org/10.18653/v1/2025.findings-acl.1165
40. Woodward, J.: What is a mechanism? a counterfactual account. Philos. Sci. **69**(S3), 366–377 (2002). https://doi.org/10.1086/341859

Integrating Decentralised AI Services in a Collaboration Ecosystem

Kerstin Sahler[(✉)] [iD], Tobias Hecking [iD], Thorsten Sommer [iD],
and Oliver Bensch [iD]

German Aerospace Center (DLR), Institute of Software Technology,
Cologne, Germany
{Kerstin.Sahler,Tobias.Hecking,Thorsten.Sommer,Oliver.Bensch}@dlr.de

Abstract. The increasing variety of generative AI systems and tools, particularly large language models, poses significant challenges for integration into larger software infrastructures due to issues with interoperability, scalability, and data protection. To address these challenges, this paper proposes a decentralised platform ecosystem that enables the composition of AI services from distributed data sources and models. The platform prioritises flexibility, scalability, re-usability, cooperation, and data protection, providing standardised interfaces and best practices for seamless collaboration among multiple stakeholders. By facilitating the creation of open, modular, and federated architectures, this ecosystem aims to unlock the full potential of AI in collaborative environments while ensuring secure data exchange and protecting sensitive information.

Keywords: Large Language Models · Retrieval-Augmented Generation · AI Software Systems

1 Introduction

Today we see an ever-growing variety of systems and tools incorporating generative AI, especially large language models (LLMs), ranging from self-hosted open source models to proprietary services. Seamless integration of AI components into larger software infrastructures imposes significant challenges in terms of interoperability, scalability, and data protection.

As a result, the development of decentralised AI services has become an increasingly important area of research, particularly in collaborative environments where multiple stakeholders and organisations need to work together. In this regard, decentralised AI service infrastructures have the potential to address the aforementioned challenges by enabling the creation of open, modular, and federated architectures that can facilitate the integration of diverse AI models and tools while ensuring secure data exchange and protecting sensitive information.

Instead of gathering data, tools, and models at a central place, in such decentralised settings, different entities maintain control over their own data and

Y. Mualla et al. (Eds.): CALM 2025, CCIS 2923, pp. 96–105, 2026.
https://doi.org/10.1007/978-3-032-20548-3_7

models while still benefiting from the collective knowledge and capabilities of the network. This approach also enables a more efficient use of resources and expertise. This, however, comes with the need for a clear definition of interfaces to ensure the interoperability of services while being lightweight such that it can be adapted by data and service providers with little additional effort.

A practical application of such a decentralised setting has been demonstrated by Bensch et al. (2025), who developed an AI assistant for the flight control team at the Columbus Control-Center of the International Space Station (ISS) [5]. Their approach integrates AI services such as an LLM with domain-specific data stored in a knowledge graph through a decentralised Retrieval-Augmented Generation (RAG) pipeline, illustrating both the potential and the technical challenges of federated AI systems.

In this paper, we demonstrate a composition of tools and concepts that eases the development of a collaborative ecosystem for building AI assistants from distributed data sources and models by defining interfaces and best practices. While our work primarily focuses on creating individual AI assistants, the architecture provides a foundation for developing agents that can participate in multi-agent systems. The ecosystem addresses the following aspects:

- **Flexibility:** Since the evolution of tools and methods is so dynamic, the platform should not impose any restrictions regarding technologies used. Instead, data or tool providing entities communicate through pre-defined interfaces but using their own methods underneath.
- **Scalability:** It must be possible that distributed storage and compute resources can be combined in an optimal way. Entities can connect new data sources or provide access to models operated on their own infrastructure at any time.
- **Re-usability:** Provided models and resources can potentially be beneficial for different use cases. To this end, the ecosystem should support the combination of existing components to new AI products.
- **Cooperation:** From the aforementioned points follows that different entities provide different resources that can be integrated through standardised interfaces. To further support collaboration, a platform is needed that allows to offer services along with proper descriptions and search options.
- **Data protection and transparency:** Data and model providers must be in full control of their data and models. The developed platform must ensure transparency about any restrictions on data usage and offer mechanisms for access control.

Therefore, the main contributions of this work are a lightweight, open-source toolbox for integrating decentralised AI services in a collaboration ecosystem that supports diverse underlying technologies and implementations, consisting of:

- A collaboration platform for creating and managing AI assistants from distributed resources.

- A Python package providing graph-based RAG algorithms.
- A unified interface for standardised context data access across distributed sources.

2   Background and Related Works

With the increasing capabilities of LLMs [6,35, *inter alia*] and their widespread acceptance, multiple approaches for integrating these models into new architectures have been proposed [7,9,25,26]. While these works primarily focus on application architectures rather than collaborative ecosystems, the work most closely related to ours is [17], which proposes standardization as a means of reducing siloed LLM app stores. However, our work goes beyond that by designing a comprehensive ecosystem architecture with concrete underlying technologies.

These technologies can be divided into three main categories: communication standards (protocols), development tools (frameworks, runtime tools, and community platforms), and orchestration tools (web and desktop applications).

Communication Standards. Examples of communication standards introduced to unify LLM access to additional context are the Model Context Protocol (MCP) [1,2] and the External Retrieval Interface (ERI) [16], which is described in detail in Sect. 3.1.

MCP is designed in a client-server architecture, comprising three key elements: the MCP host, MCP client, and MCP server. The MCP host is an LLM application that implements the MCP client, which handles communication with MCP servers. MCP servers enable the integration of data, tools, and prompts from local or remote sources. While MCP improves flexibility and scalability in AI assistant development, it can introduce different security threats throughout its lifecycle [18].

Development Tools. Tools that support the development of LLM-based applications can be divided into three sub-categories: frameworks, runtime tools, and community platforms.

As a framework, LangChain [21,22] provides a structured development environment to integrate models, tools, and data when developing AI-based applications through an open source library, simplifying the development process but constraining its flexibility by predefined methods and abstractions.

Runtime tools, on the other hand, focus on model execution. Examples include llama.cpp [13], Ollama [30,31], and vLLM [20], which offer lightweight solutions for local LLM inference through accessible interfaces, facilitating the integration of LLMs into orchestration tools and efficient model deployment.

Community platforms like Hugging Face [19], support developers by providing a platform for sharing datasets and a wide range of models, leveraging runtime tools such as llama.cpp or its own transformer library. In addition, Hugging Face increases knowledge exchange through blogs, articles, and discussions, strengthening its collaborative features. However, unlike decentralised approaches, the platform requires users to upload their models and data to centralised repositories, which limits user control over their data and reduces the scalability due to data and model duplication across the ecosystem. Hugging Face's focus is on machine learning, making additional orchestration and customization for RAG systems inevitable.

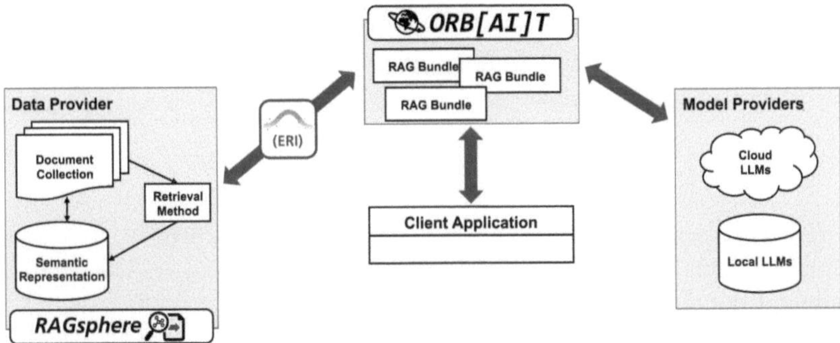

Fig. 1. High-level depiction of the proposed architecture (Adapted from Hecking et al. (2025) [16]).

Orchestration Tools. Orchestration tools serve as intermediaries between users, different LLMs, and additional context information and can be implemented either as web or desktop applications.

As web-based platforms, LibreChat [3,24] and Open WebUI [4,32] facilitate resource sharing between platform users, but also introduce potential security threats. Open WebUI addresses these risks through group-based access control that restricts resource access to different user categories. Both web applications enable the development of AI assistants, emphasizing the reusability of components. Still, in both tools, models can only be added by administrators, and additional data is integrated through local file uploads using the application's built-in retrieval methods, limiting its flexibility. Nevertheless, LibreChat supports MCP integration with a focus on tool usage, offering a workaround for remote data integration.

Desktop applications, in contrast, provide enhanced security by default since resources are not shared among users, though this approach limits cooperation possibilities. Several desktop applications such as LM Studio [11,12] and AnythingLLM [27,28] support MCP for the integration of external context, while MindWork AI Studio [33] utilises ERI. Both techniques strengthen flexibility and scalability. Component reusability, on the other hand, varies across these applications, with AnythingLLM offering agent creation capabilities based on available resources, AI Studio providing only built-in assistants for specific tasks, and no support for component combination in LM Studio.

3   Proposed Architecture

Our decentralised ecosystem is based on the architecture introduced by Hecking et al. (2025) [16]. As illustrated in Fig. 1, participating entities include model providers offering access to LLMs through runtime tools and data providers implementing interfaces for data retrieval from knowledge bases. Both providers are connected through Orb[AI]t, a registry platform for data, models, and RAG bundles (details are provided in Sect. 3.3) that enables searching and combining services across entities through a common interface. The following section details the architectural components.

3.1   External Retrieval Interface

RAG [23] is a common pattern for adapting LLMs to specific use cases and reducing hallucinations by fetching relevant documents from knowledge bases to provide additional context for answer generation.

ERI[1] allows for decentralised RAG implementation where LLM deployment, data retrieval, and context augmentation are handled by different entities. ERI defines communication rules and provides standardised connections between data providers, model providers, and interaction platforms (e.g., Orb[AI]t or Mind-Work AI Studio) using a client-server architecture based on OpenAPI [34].

The data provider acts as the ERI server, while the interaction platform serves as the client. The client forwards the user query and chat history to the server, which triggers retrieval and returns the relevant context. The platform then augments the query with this context and directs the resulting prompt to the model for generation. This allows data providers to implement custom retrieval logic independently of the interaction platform.

Consequently, the data remain with the providers in contrast to central storage, ensuring data sovereignty. In addition, ERI enables providers to specify data security levels including authentication methods (e.g., username/password, token, etc.) or model restrictions like limiting highly sensitive data to local models only. This approach provides flexibility in deployment of models by emphasising local processing for sensitive data while supporting external for non-sensitive operations, recognising data protection involves multiple complementary techniques for ensuring privacy, confidentiality, and security. The interaction platform maintains visual transparency about such restrictions and implements the data security requirements.

3.2   RAGsphere

To ease the development of RAG applications with ERI conforming data sources, we developed *RAGsphere*[2], a Python library supporting various retrieval and indexing methods with a focus on graph retrieval. This framework splits RAG

---

[1] https://github.com/MindWorkAI/ERI.
[2] https://github.com/DLR-SC/RAG-Sphere/.

into "Indexing" and "Retrieval" stages, allowing users to select predefined configuration or combinations across methods, independent of the underlying database system.

In addition to classical RAG, RAGsphere implements graph-based methods, including GraphRAG [10], LightRAG [14], and PathRAG [8]. We also introduce "Naive GraphRAG", where communities identified by GraphRAG are indexed into a vector database during indexing. Then, the user query is matched against the database during retrieval instead of querying the LLM for each summary. This optimisation reduces the answer generation time, depending on graph size and number of communities and sub-communities.

3.3   Orb[AI]t

Orb[AI]t[3] (pronounced as "orbit", /'ɔːbɪt/) serves as a central registry of models and ERI data connections to facilitate exchange and cooperation between decentralised entities. Many of the requirements can already be fulfilled by a custom configuration of Open WebUI [15,29]. It incorporates four main sections: models, data, bundles, and prompts. Each section provides a searchable catalogue with resource cards containing detailed descriptions and tags for filtering. The original Open WebUI implementation has been modified to be able to incorporate ERI connections to interface with external retrieval systems instead of uploading date directly. This makes it possible to fully implement the distributed RAG system outlined above.

Models. Displays the models available to the user through Ollama connections, keeping models with providers instead of being uploaded centrally, efficiently exploiting resources in decentralised organisations. The model upload functionality is extended to all users rather than being limited to platform administrators.

Data. Extends the knowledge section of Open WebUI by connecting ERI server endpoints. As a data provider can offer multiple data sources, each combination of data source and retrieval method creates an individual entry.

RAG Bundles. Users can configure whole RAG systems, called RAG bundles, by combining models, data, and prompts (see Fig. 2). Thereby, users create shareable AI assistants tailored for specific tasks. For example, a user can create an assistant with a specially aligned model for a specific task with complementary data and an optimised prompt. Open WebUI already provides most of this functionality but the functionality to use external retrieval systems via ERI had to be added.

Prompts. Derived from Open WebUI, the prompt section enables saving and sharing effective natural language prompts, reducing re-entering prompts for recurring tasks and time-consuming prompt engineering.

---

[3] https://github.com/DLR-SC/orb-ai-t

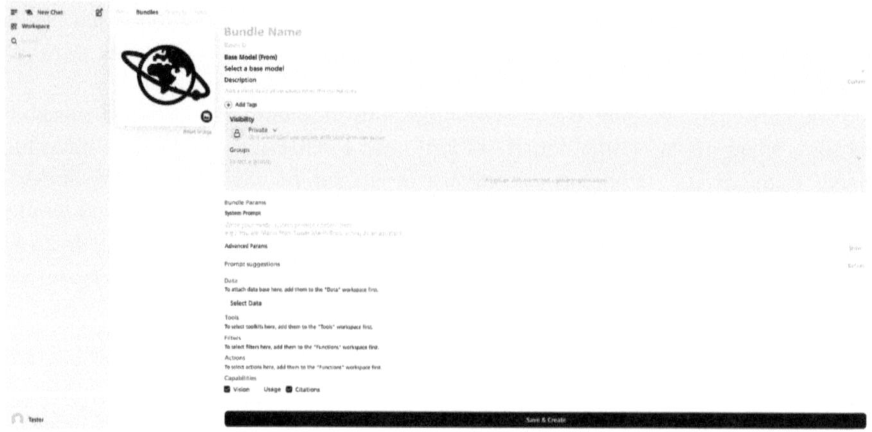

Fig. 2. Except from the Orb[AI]t platform highlighting the feature to create RAG bundles.

Groups. Individual access to models, data, bundles, and prompts can be specified by the provider, distinguishing between two distinct states: *public* or *private*. Public entries are accessible to all users, while private entries are only accessible to a selected group of users. These groups can either be formed by the provider or derived from existing organisational groups. RAG bundles inherit the strictest privacy settings from their components.

Additional Features. Beyond the core features, Orb[AI]t offers a *forum* to further encourage cooperation by enabling users to engage in topic-related discussions. An additional *chat* interface provides a testing environment for different data-models combinations. However, the focus of Orb[AI]t is on building complete AI systems rather than direct user-model communication.

3.4   Integration in Desktop Applications

Companies with centrally managed workstations often favour desktop solutions for generative AI. MindWork AI Studio [33] offers a viable open-source option, supporting centralised rollout and flexible configuration management for individual groups, departments, or organisation-wide. Unlike web-applications, desktop applications offer a higher level of data protection as all interactions with the AI system are stored locally on the employee's device instead of storing chat histories or similar information on external servers. Additionally, desktop applications can interact directly with the user's file system, thus directories with documents can be embedded for RAG, and generative AI can directly edit these documents.

To ensure compatibility with our ecosystem, we propose a two-step implementation for RAG bundles to desktop applications. First, Orb[AI]t offers an export function, which generates a downloadable JSON file that contains all relevant data. Second, desktop applications can read and adapt these data structures. For example, MindWork AI Studio uses the exported RAG bundle to create a respective assistant.

For a simpler long-term implementation, we propose a custom protocol handler for deep linking. This widely-used technology enables seamless app integration. For example, when a user clicks on the app recommendations on a website, the app store opens displaying the relevant app. Similarly, users can identify suitable RAG bundles on the Orb[AI]t platform and, with a simple interaction, start the desktop application and initiate the import process. Implementing a custom protocol handler requires developers to define an appropriate URI scheme. We suggest `rag-bundle`. Compatible software can register with the operating system to become available as a target for interaction.

4   Discussion and Conclusion

In this paper, we described our ecosystem for quick development and integration of decentralised AI services. It is built on top of established tools and platforms but puts strong emphasis on loose coupling of services and the distributed collaboration between data and model providing entities. This is achieved by the definition of lightweight interfaces such as ERI that can be adopted to existing data infrastructures with little effort but enable a standardised way of data exchange. The Orb[AI]t platform allows finding, orchestrating, and publishing of services. However, instead of being a central repository to push data and host models, it is rather a means to find and orchestrate different services that are operated elsewhere, leaving full control to the respective data and model providers. In future works, we will especially work on better support of multi-agent systems and tool usage. To this end, it is planned to extend the concept of RAG bundles to enable more complex interactions between services, and to provide an extended ERI implementation.

References

1. Anthropic: model context protocol: connect your AI applications to the world (2025). https://modelcontextprotocol.io/
2. Anthropic, Open Source Community: Model Context Protocol: An open protocol that enables seamless integration between LLM applications and external data sources and tools (2025). https://github.com/modelcontextprotocol
3. Avila, D.: Open Source Community: LibreChat (2025). https://github.com/danny-avila/LibreChat
4. Baek, T.J.: Open Source Community: Open WebUI (2025). https://github.com/open-webui/open-webui
5. Bensch, O., et al.: Enhancing operations at the columbus control-center: a hybrid approach utilizing large language models, knowledge graphs, and retrieval-augmented generation. In: Proceedings of the 76th International Astronautical Congress (IAC). International Astronautical Federation (IAF), Sydney, Australia (2025)

6. Brown, T., et al.: Language models are few-shot learners. Adv. Neural. Inf. Process. Syst. **33**, 1877–1901 (2020)
7. Bucaioni, A., Weyssow, M., He, J., Lyu, Y., Lo, D.: A functional software reference architecture for LLM-integrated systems. In: 2025 IEEE 22nd International Conference on Software Architecture Companion (ICSA-C), pp. 1–5. IEEE (2025)
8. Chen, B., et al.: PathRAG: pruning graph-based retrieval augmented generation with relational paths (2025). https://arxiv.org/abs/2502.14902
9. Chuang, C.C., Chen, K.C.: Retrieval augmented generation on hybrid cloud: a new architecture for knowledge base systems. In: 2024 16th IIAI International Congress on Advanced Applied Informatics (IIAI-AAI), pp. 68–71. IEEE (2024)
10. Edge, D., et al.: From local to global: a graph RAG approach to query-focused summarization (2025). https://arxiv.org/abs/2404.16130
11. Element Labs: LM Studio (2025). https://github.com/lmstudio-ai
12. Element Labs: LM Studio: Your local AI toolkit (2025). https://lmstudio.ai/
13. Gerganov, G.: Open Source Community: llama.cpp (2025). https://github.com/ggml-org/llama.cpp
14. Guo, Z., Xia, L., Yu, Y., Ao, T., Huang, C.: LightRAG: simple and fast retrieval-augmented generation (2025). https://arxiv.org/abs/2410.05779
15. Haefliger, S., Von Krogh, G., Spaeth, S.: Code reuse in open source software. Manage. Sci. **54**(1), 180–193 (2008)
16. Hecking, T., Sommer, T., Felderer, M.: An architecture and protocol for decentralized retrieval augmented generation. In: 2025 IEEE 22nd International Conference on Software Architecture Companion (ICSA-C), pp. 31–35. IEEE (2025)
17. Hou, X., Zhao, Y., Wang, H.: The next frontier of LLM applications: open ecosystems and hardware synergy. arXiv preprint arXiv:2503.04596 (2025)
18. Hou, X., Zhao, Y., Wang, S., Wang, H.: Model Context Protocol (MCP): landscape, security threats, and future research directions. arXiv preprint arXiv:2503.23278 (2025)
19. Hugging Face: Hugging Face – The AI community building the future (2025). https://huggingface.co/
20. Kwon, W., et al.: Efficient memory management for large language model serving with pagedattention. In: Proceedings of the ACM SIGOPS 29th Symposium on Operating Systems Principles (2023)
21. LangChain: LangChain: The platform for reliable agents (2025). https://github.com/langchain-ai/langchain
22. LangChain, Open Source Community: LangChain: Build context-aware, reasoning applications with LangChain's flexible abstractions and AI-first toolkits (2025). https://github.com/langchain-ai/langchain
23. Lewis, P., et al.: Retrieval-augmented generation for knowledge-intensive NLP tasks. In: Larochelle, H., Ranzato, M., Hadsell, R., Balcan, M., Lin, H. (eds.) Advances in Neural Information Processing Systems. vol. 33, pp. 9459–9474. Curran Associates, Inc. (2020). https://proceedings.neurips.cc/paper_files/paper/2020/file/6b493230205f780e1bc26945df7481e5-Paper.pdf
24. LibreChat: LibreChat: Unify AI Power (2025). https://www.librechat.ai/
25. Lu, Q., Zhu, L., Xu, X., Xing, Z., Harrer, S., Whittle, J.: Towards responsible generative AI: a reference architecture for designing foundation model based agents. In: 2024 IEEE 21st International Conference on Software Architecture Companion (ICSA-C), pp. 119–126. IEEE (2024)
26. Lu, Q., Zhu, L., Xu, X., Xing, Z., Whittle, J.: Towards responsible AI in the era of generative AI: a reference architecture for designing foundation model based systems. IEEE Software (2024)

27. Mintplex Labs: AnythingLLM: The all-in-one AI application (2025). https://anythingllm.com/
28. Mintplex Labs, Open Source Community: AnythingLLM (2025). https://github.com/Mintplex-Labs/anything-llm
29. Mohagheghi, P., Conradi, R.: Quality, productivity and economic benefits of software reuse: a review of industrial studies. Empir. Softw. Eng. **12**(5), 471–516 (2007)
30. Ollama: Ollama: Get up and running with large language models (2025). https://ollama.com/
31. Ollama, Open Source Community: Ollama (2025). https://github.com/ollama/ollama
32. Open WebUI: Open WebUI (2025). https://openwebui.com/
33. Sommer, T.: Open Source Community: MindWork AI Studio (2025). https://github.com/MindWorkAI/AI-Studio
34. The Linux Foundation: OpenAPI Initiative: The world's most widely used API description standard (2025). https://www.openapis.org/
35. Zhao, W.X., et al.: A survey of large language models. arXiv preprint arXiv:2303.18223 (2023)

A Hybrid Metaheuristic-Guided Multi-Agent Reinforcement Learning Framework for Cooperative Unsignalized Intersection Coordination

Fatima-Zahrae El-Qoraychy$^{(\boxtimes)}$ [ID], Mahjoub Dridi [ID],
and Jean-Charles Créput [ID]

Université de Technologie de Belfort Montbéliard, UTBM, CIAD UR 7533,
F-90010 Belfort, France
`fatima.el-qoraychy@utbm.fr`

Abstract. Learning to coordinate multiple autonomous agents remains a central challenge in artificial intelligence, particularly in dynamic and partially observable environments. Multi-Agent Reinforcement Learning (MARL) offers a promising paradigm for such distributed decision-making, yet its training process often suffers from non-stationarity, unstable convergence, and reward misalignment between individual and collective rewards. These issues are amplified in safety-critical domains, such as the coordination of Connected and Autonomous Vehicles (CAVs) at unsignalized intersections, where agents must negotiate right-of-way decisions under uncertainty. This paper proposes a hybrid framework that combines MARL, implemented via the Twin Delayed Deep Deterministic Policy Gradient (TD3) algorithm, with a metaheuristic optimization supervisor acting as an adaptive reward modulator. The metaheuristic component dynamically tunes the reward-function coefficients during training, effectively reshaping the causal relationships between agent actions and global outcomes. This adaptive calibration enhances learning stability, promotes cooperative behaviors, and accelerates convergence across agents that follow a Centralized Training and Decentralized Execution (CTDE) scheme, thus enabling adaptation and stable coordination in multi-agent traffic systems.

Keywords: CAV coordination · Unsignalized intersections ·
Multi-agent reinforcement learning · Metaheuristic

1 Introduction

The rapid evolution of Connected and Autonomous Vehicles (CAVs) has reshaped the landscape of intelligent transportation, enabling unprecedented opportunities to improve traffic efficiency and safety [14,24]. However, a persistent challenge lies in the real-time coordination of CAVs at unsignalized intersections, where the absence of traditional traffic lights requires autonomous agents

Y. Mualla et al. (Eds.): CALM 2025, CCIS 2923, pp. 106–118, 2026.
https://doi.org/10.1007/978-3-032-20548-3_8

to make sequential and cooperative decisions under uncertainty [19]. In these contexts, vehicles must continuously negotiate right-of-way, optimize crossing sequences, and ensure collision-free trajectories, a task that becomes increasingly complex as the traffic density and the number of intersections grow [8,12,17].

Several research directions have been explored to address this challenge. Rule-based strategies, such as First-Come-First-Served (FCFS) or reservation-based protocols [20,21], offer simplicity and formal safety guarantees but suffer from limited scalability and suboptimal throughput in dense traffic. Optimization-based methods, including metaheuristic algorithms such as Particle Swarm Optimization (PSO), have demonstrated the ability to compute near-optimal coordination plans. Yet, their computational complexity and lack of adaptability to dynamic traffic flows restrict their use in real-time decision-making [1,4,5,10,11]. In parallel, Reinforcement Learning (RL) has emerged as a powerful paradigm for autonomous decision-making in dynamic environments [7,16]. In particular, Multi-Agent Reinforcement Learning (MARL) extends RL to multi-agent systems, allowing each agent (vehicle or intersection manager) to learn adaptive policies through interaction with its environment and neighboring agents. MARL has been successfully applied to traffic signal control, adaptive platooning, and conflict resolution at unsignalized intersections [2,22,25,27]. Despite these successes, MARL still faces critical challenges such as hyperparameter sensitivity, reward misalignment, slow convergence, and instability during training, especially in multi-intersection or mixed-traffic settings [3,13,15]. These limitations arise from the non-stationarity of multi-agent environments and the high dimensionality of continuous action spaces.

To address these limitations, recent studies have turned toward the hybridization of RL with metaheuristic optimization techniques, an emerging research field that combines the adaptability of learning with the global search capabilities of metaheuristics. Hybrid approaches can enhance exploration, balance multiple objectives, and dynamically tune key hyperparameters such as learning rates, discount factors, or reward weights [18]. By leveraging population-based search and stochastic optimization, metaheuristics such as PSO, Genetic Algorithms (GA), Grey Wolf Optimizer (GWO), and Ant Colony Optimization (ACO) have been successfully used to improve the stability and performance of RL models across various domains [9,18,23,26]. This synergy has given rise to the broader concept of Metaheuristic-Enhanced Reinforcement Learning (MHRL), which aims to bridge the gap between global optimization and adaptive decision-making.

Building on this paradigm, this paper proposes a novel hybrid MARL framework integrating TD3 with a metaheuristic supervisor for dynamic reward adaptation. The key insight is to regulate the learning behavior of MARL agents not by altering their architectures, but by optimizing the reward-function coefficients $(\lambda_1, \ldots, \lambda_5)$ using a metaheuristic algorithm. This dynamic tuning aligns the agents' local objectives with the global performance goals, balancing safety, efficiency, and comfort across multiple intersections. The TD3 algorithm provides stable continuous control of vehicle accelerations under the Centralized Training and Decentralized Execution (CTDE) paradigm, while the metaheuristic supervisor ensures adaptive reward shaping and faster convergence. Even small causal perturbations introduced by the metaheuristic in the reward-function coefficients can significantly influence the convergence trajectory of the MARL agents, leading to more stable and efficient coordination.

The rest of this paper is organized as follows: Sect. 2 introduces the proposed hybrid framework that combines MARL with a metaheuristic optimization layer under the TD3 algorithm and the CTDE paradigm. Sect. 3 presents a theoretical analysis and discusses the main properties, advantages, and potential limitations of the proposed framework, while also outlining open research directions and possible extensions to broader contexts such as mixed-traffic and hierarchical coordination. Finally, Sect. 4 concludes the paper and highlights perspectives for large-scale deployment and future research avenues.

2   Methodology

This section presents our hybrid framework for multi-agent coordination of CAVs in networks of unsignalized intersections. The proposed method integrates MARL based on the Twin Delayed Deep Deterministic Policy Gradient (TD3) algorithm, with a metaheuristic optimization supervisor that dynamically tunes the reward function parameters to improve convergence and performance. The design follows a Centralized Training with Decentralized Execution (CTDE) paradigm, ensuring scalability and adaptability across multiple intersections.

2.1   Problem Formulation

In multi-intersection traffic networks, control decisions made by one intersection directly affect the flow conditions at neighboring intersections due to temporal and spatial coupling. Therefore, effective coordination requires a hierarchical learning strategy capable of handling distributed decision-making under uncertainty.

In the proposed framework, each agent corresponds to an intersection manager that controls the longitudinal acceleration of vehicles within its local area. The agents cooperate through information sharing about vehicle positions and flow conditions. A centralized critic observes the global state during training, capturing cross-intersection dependencies, while each intersection manager deploys a local actor for independent execution. This architecture allows decentralized operation while maintaining global consistency. The objective is to jointly optimize vehicle trajectories to:

- maximize throughput across the network,
- minimize average waiting and travel times,
- ensure safety in conflict zones,
- maintain comfort (smooth acceleration profiles),
- and guarantee fairness among competing approaches.

We model this coordination problem as a Multi-Agent Markov Decision Process (MAMDP), where each agent seeks to improve local performance while contributing to network-level efficiency.

2.2 Multi-Agent MDP Formulation

The coordination problem is modeled as a Multi-Agent Markov Decision Process (MAMDP), defined by the tuple:

$$\mathcal{M} = \langle \mathcal{I}, \mathcal{S}, \{\mathcal{O}_i\}_{i\in\mathcal{I}}, \{\mathcal{A}_i\}_{i\in\mathcal{I}}, P, \{R_i\}_{i\in\mathcal{I}}, \gamma \rangle,$$

where:

- $\mathcal{I} = \{1, 2, \ldots, M\}$ denotes the set of agents, each representing an unsignalized intersection manager;
- $\mathcal{S}$ is the global state space capturing the joint configuration of all intersections and vehicles;
- $\mathcal{O}_i \subset \mathcal{S}$ is the local observation available to agent i, including only information about its local intersection;
- $\mathcal{A}_i$ is the continuous action space of agent i, corresponding to the control decisions (e.g., vehicle accelerations) within its area of responsibility;
- $P : \mathcal{S} \times \mathcal{A}_1 \times \cdots \times \mathcal{A}_M \to \mathcal{S}$ is the transition function describing the joint system dynamics;
- $R_i : \mathcal{S} \times \mathcal{A}_i \to \mathbb{R}$ is the local reward function of agent i;
- $\gamma \in (0, 1]$ is the discount factor controlling the temporal horizon of each agent's objective.

Each agent i aims to learn a deterministic policy $\pi_i : \mathcal{O}_i \to \mathcal{A}_i$ that maximizes its expected cumulative discounted reward:

$$J_i(\pi_i) = \mathbb{E}_{s_0, a_t^i \sim \pi_i}\left[\sum_{t=0}^{\infty} \gamma^t R_i(s_t, a_t^i)\right].$$

Because the control space is continuous and the interactions among agents are strongly coupled, the MAMDP formulation is particularly suited to continuous-action algorithms such as TD3 [6].

In the proposed framework, a shared centralized critic leverages the global state $\mathcal{S}$ and joint action set $\mathcal{A}$ during training to guide gradient updates and mitigate the non-stationarity induced by concurrent policy learning. During execution, each intersection manager relies solely on its local actor π_i and local observation $\mathcal{O}_i$, ensuring decentralized, real-time, and scalable decision-making under the CTDE paradigm. Figure 1 illustrates the overall architecture.

2.3 State Representation

At each time step t, each intersection manager observes the local traffic state represented by the vehicles under its control. The state vector of each vehicle j is defined as:

$$s_j(t) = [x_j(t), y_j(t), v_j(t), d_i, \ell_j, a_j(t)],$$

where:

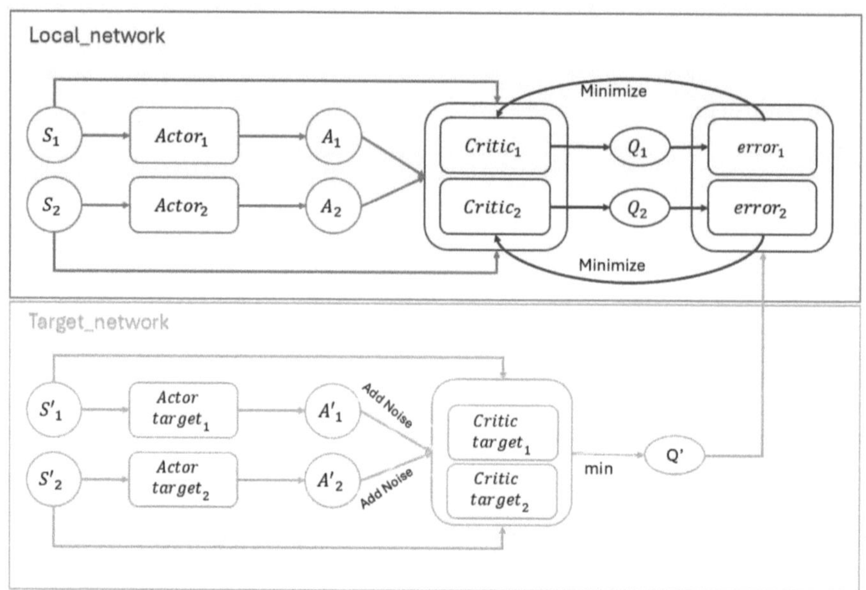

Fig. 1. Centralized Training and Decentralized Execution (CTDE) architecture of the proposed Multi-Agent TD3 framework. Each intersection manager acts locally using its individual actor network, while a centralized critic stabilizes training using global state information.

- (x_j, y_j): position of vehicle i, normalized by lane length,
- $v_j(t)$: normalized velocity,
- d_j: intended maneuver (left, right, straight),
- ℓ_j: lane identifier,
- $a_j(t)$: current acceleration.

The overall state of an intersection manager is a concatenation of all vehicle states within its control zone:

$$S_t = [s_1(t), s_2(t), \ldots, s_n(t)],$$

where n is the number of controlled vehicles. Normalization to the range $[-1, 1]$ ensures scale invariance and stabilizes learning.

2.4   Action Space

Each intersection manager outputs a continuous vector of accelerations for the vehicles within its zone:

$$A_t = [a_1(t), a_2(t), \ldots, a_n(t)], \quad a_j(t) \in [-1, 1].$$

Each normalized action $a_j(t)$ is mapped to a real-world acceleration:

$$a_j^{\text{real}}(t) = a_{\min} + \frac{a_j(t) + 1}{2}(a_{\max} - a_{\min}),$$

where $a_{\min} = -4$ m/s^2 and $a_{\max} = 2$ m/s^2. These bounds reflect the physical constraints of vehicle dynamics and ensure comfortable, collision-free motion.

2.5 Reward Function and Constraints

The reward function plays a fundamental role in RL, as it defines the optimization signal that drives agent behavior and encodes the system's global objectives. In multi-agent traffic coordination, the reward acts as a causal driver of policy adaptation. It determines how each agent interprets environmental feedback, balances competing objectives, and shapes its long-term strategy through trial and error. A poorly designed reward function can therefore lead to unstable or unsafe learning outcomes, regardless of the underlying algorithm. To explicitly quantify the performance of each intersection manager in balancing safety, efficiency, comfort, and fairness, the local reward at each step is defined as:

$$r_i(t) = \lambda_1 EN(t) - \lambda_2 WT(t) - \lambda_3 CN(t) - \lambda_4 J(t) + \lambda_5 F(t),$$

where:

- $EN(t)$: number of vehicles evacuated at time step t,
- $WT(t)$: total waiting time of all vehicles at time step t,
- $CN(t)$: collision indicator (severe penalty) at time step t,
- $J(t)$: jerk measure penalizing abrupt acceleration changes at time step t,
- $F(t)$: fairness term reducing disparity in waiting times across flows at time step t.

The coefficients $(\lambda_1, \ldots, \lambda_5)$ govern the trade-off between safety, efficiency, and comfort. Their inappropriate setting can severely degrade performance, leading to unsafe or inefficient behaviors. Because the reward coefficients $(\lambda_1, \ldots, \lambda_5)$ directly determine how each agent prioritizes conflicting objectives, even small variations in their values can causally alter the policy gradients, the exploration behavior, and ultimately the convergence path of the MARL system. This strong causal sensitivity makes manual or static tuning impractical, as fixed coefficients may drive the agents toward unsafe or inefficient equilibria. Therefore, a metaheuristic optimization layer is introduced to adaptively adjust these coefficients during training, discovering reward configurations that causally lead to stable and balanced learning dynamics across intersections.

2.6 Metaheuristic Supervision and Hybrid Integration

The metaheuristic optimization layer functions as a supervisory mechanism that continuously guides the MARL training process by adaptively tuning the reward-function coefficients $\boldsymbol{\lambda} = (\lambda_1, \lambda_2, \lambda_3, \lambda_4, \lambda_5)$. Rather than relying on static or manually defined weights, the metaheuristic component explores candidate configurations of $\boldsymbol{\lambda}$ that balance multiple, and often competing, traffic objectives across all intersections. Consequently, the reward function becomes an *adaptive control signal* that dynamically aligns local agent incentives with global system performance.

To achieve this, the proposed hybrid framework operates under a **two-level optimization hierarchy**, integrating both an offline and an online metaheuristic process.

Offline Phase: Before MARL training, the metaheuristic optimizer evaluates candidate reward coefficients λ by performing short preliminary training episodes. This offline evaluation does not involve full policy convergence; it only assesses whether a candidate configuration can lead to stable and effective learning. Each optimization cycle evaluates a population of candidate vectors λ over short preliminary episodes using a normalized fitness function (see Eq. 1), and selects the configuration that maximizes overall performance. This phase provides a robust initialization and consistent early learning.

Online Phase: During MARL training, the system enters the online optimization phase. Agents actively interact with the environment and continuously update their policies in real time, adapting their behavior based on immediate feedback. Using the offline-optimal $\lambda^\star$ as a baseline, each agent i periodically introduces small, controlled perturbations $\delta_j(t)$ at each simulation step t. The effective reward for agent i is then expressed as:

$$
\begin{aligned}
r_i^{\text{eff}}(t) = {} & (\lambda_1^\star + \delta_1(t)) \cdot EN_i(t) - (\lambda_2^\star + \delta_2(t)) \cdot WT_i(t) \\
& - (\lambda_3^\star + \delta_3(t)) \cdot C_i(t) - (\lambda_4^\star + \delta_4(t)) \cdot J_i(t) \\
& + (\lambda_5^\star + \delta_5(t)) \cdot F_i(t),
\end{aligned}
$$

where $\delta_j(t)$ represents small perturbations derived from short-term feedback on local performance metrics (e.g., waiting time, or safety indicators). These perturbations are constrained to maintain the global reward structure while promoting exploration and adaptation, thus preventing agents from being trapped in suboptimal equilibria and accelerating convergence toward globally efficient behaviors. The overall hybrid framework, combining offline metaheuristic optimization with online MARL and local reward perturbations, is summarized in Algorithm 1.

Fitness Evaluation. To consistently evaluate candidate reward coefficients, all performance metrics m are first normalized to the range $[0, 1]$ using the general formula:

$$
f_m = \begin{cases}
\min\left(\frac{V_m}{V_m^*}, 1\right), & \text{if metric } m \text{ is to be maximized,} \\
\min\left(\frac{V_m^*}{V_m}, 1\right), & \text{if metric } m \text{ is to be minimized,}
\end{cases}
$$

where V_m is the observed value of metric m (e.g., Waiting time, Delay, Collisions, Jerk, Fairness) and V_m^* is the desired or target value.

The overall fitness of a candidate reward coefficient vector λ is then computed as the average over all M normalized metrics:

$$\mathcal{F}(\lambda) = \frac{1}{M} \sum_{m=1}^{M} f_m. \tag{1}$$

This normalization ensures that all metrics contribute comparably to the overall fitness, enabling fair and robust evaluation during both offline and online optimization.

Algorithm 1: Hybrid TD3–Metaheuristic framework (final version)

---

1 **Initialize:** individual actor networks θ_i for each agent i, twin critics ϕ_1, ϕ_2, target networks $\theta'_i, \phi'_1, \phi'_2$, and replay buffer $\mathcal{D}$

2 **Offline phase: metaheuristic search of reward weights**
3 Generate a population of candidate λ values
4 Evaluate each candidate over a few episodes using TD3 training Select the best $\lambda^\star$ according to fitness $\mathcal{F}(\lambda)$

5 **Online phase: MARL with local reward variations**
6 **for** *each episode e* **do**
7   Reset environment and get initial observations O
8   **for** *each time step t within episode e* **do**
9   **for** *each agent i* **do**
10   Compute action $a_i = \pi_{\theta_i}(o_i)$
11   Compute small perturbations $\delta_j(t)$
12   Compute effective reward $r_i^{\text{eff}}(t)$ using $\lambda^\star + \delta(t)$
13   Step environment, observe next state O'
14   Store $(O, A, R^{\text{eff}}(t), O')$ in buffer $\mathcal{D}$
15         $O \leftarrow O'$
16   Update critics ϕ_1, ϕ_2 and actors θ_i per TD3 rules

17 **Deployment phase:** freeze θ_i and $\lambda^\star$; run decentralized control in real time

---

3 Theoretical Analysis and Discussion

The proposed hybrid MARL–metaheuristic framework, as illustrated in Fig. 2, provides a unified view of the interaction between the TD3 learning layer, the metaheuristic reward optimizer, and the traffic environment. It introduces several theoretical advantages compared to conventional MARL or optimization approaches:

- **Reward-Level Adaptation:** By directly tuning the reward-function coefficients $(\lambda_1, \ldots, \lambda_5)$, the metaheuristic supervisor continuously reshapes the optimization landscape faced by TD3 agents. This dynamic reward calibration aligns short-term agent incentives with long-term system objectives, mitigating common MARL issues such as reward imbalance and conflicting learning signals.

- **Stabilized Learning Dynamics:** Online adaptation of the reward parameters prevents gradient oscillations and policy divergence, two frequent problems in continuous multi-agent TD3 settings. By evaluating the fitness of reward configurations across short training intervals, the metaheuristic acts as a feedback controller that regulates policy updates toward stable convergence.
- **Scalability Across Multiple Intersections:** The CTDE structure, combined with metaheuristic supervision, ensures consistent learning as the number of agents increases. Centralized critics capture cross-intersection dependencies, while decentralized actors maintain low computational cost and local autonomy.
- **Adaptive Trade-off Management:** The metaheuristic layer autonomously balances conflicting objectives (throughput, safety, comfort) in real time. This adaptability is particularly valuable under dynamic or congested traffic regimes where fixed weighting coefficients would otherwise degrade performance.

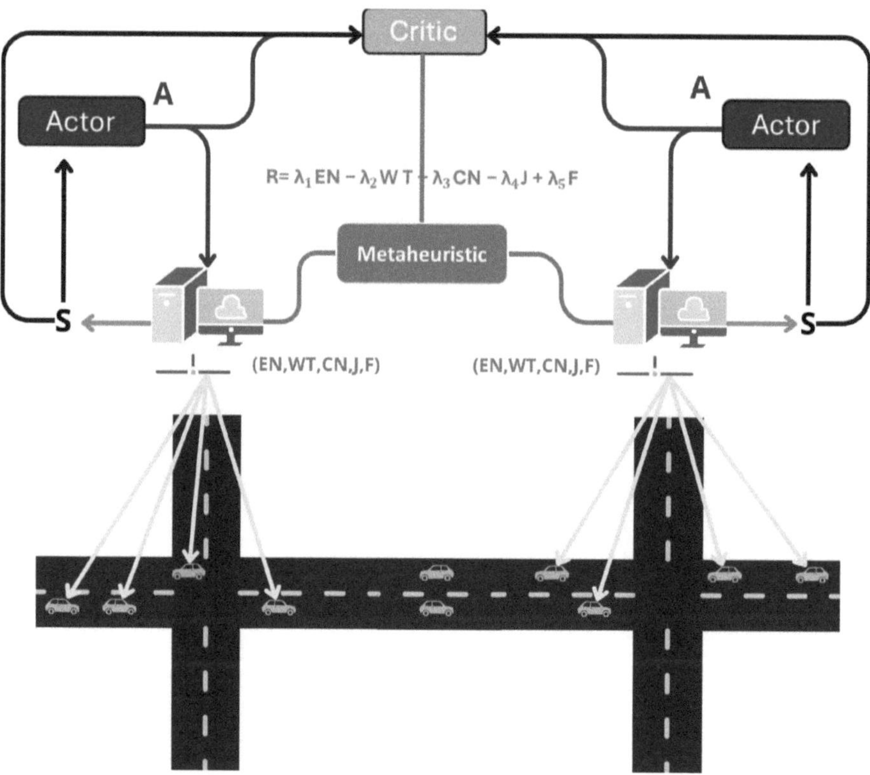

Fig. 2. Global architecture of the proposed hybrid MARLâĂŞMetaheuristic framework under CTDE paradigm.

- **Causal and Theoretical Convergence Support:** While TD3 guarantees monotonic policy improvement under bounded Q-value estimation error, the metaheuristic feedback loop reduces the variance of reward gradients across agents. This acts as a causal regularization mechanism that enhances empirical convergence speed and cross-agent consistency.

3.1 Complexity and Scalability Analysis

The hybrid framework maintains polynomial computational complexity with respect to the number of intersections M and vehicles per intersection N. Let $O(T_{TD3})$ denote the cost of one TD3 update and $O(T_{meta})$ the cost of one metaheuristic iteration. The per-episode complexity can be expressed as:

$$O(T_{\text{total}}) = O(M \cdot T_{TD3}) + O(T_{meta}),$$

where $T_{meta} \ll M \cdot T_{TD3}$ since the metaheuristic operates asynchronously and at a lower frequency. This structure ensures that execution time remains acceptable as the network scales up.

3.2 Limitations and Challenges

Despite its advantages, the proposed framework also presents several open challenges:

- **Computational Overhead:** Although the metaheuristic operates at coarse intervals, evaluating multiple reward configurations increases training time. Surrogate modeling or incremental evaluation strategies could mitigate this cost.
- **Metaheuristic Parameter Sensitivity:** The performance still depends on metaheuristic settings (e.g., swarm size, crossover rate). Adaptive metaheuristics capable of self-tuning these parameters represent a promising research direction.
- **Transferability Across Scenarios:** The optimal reward configuration for one network may not generalize to others. Techniques such as domain randomization and transfer learning could improve robustness.

3.3 Open Research Directions

The hybrid design opens multiple avenues for further investigation:

- **Mixed-Traffic and Human-in-the-Loop Scenarios:** Extend the framework to heterogeneous environments with both CAVs and human-driven vehicles. This would require policies that handle uncertainty, partial cooperation, and explainable decision-making.

- **Causal and Explainable Multi-Agent Learning:** Investigate how causal inference techniques and explainable AI (XAI) models can be integrated into the MARLâĂŞmetaheuristic framework to make agents' behaviors interpretable. For instance, causal graphs or attention-based saliency maps could be used to analyze how changes in λ or agent interactions influence emergent coordination strategies.
- **Hierarchical Multi-Agent Coordination:** Explore multi-level architectures where upper-layer controllers coordinate groups of intersections, while local TD3 agents handle low-level acceleration control. Such a hierarchy could incorporate causal reasoning between intersections to improve network-level cooperation.
- **Formal Robustness and Convergence Analysis:** Derive theoretical guarantees on convergence bounds, stability, and safety under bounded exploration noise and periodic metaheuristic updates.

4   Conclusion

This paper introduces a hybrid MARL framework that integrates TD3 with a metaheuristic reward optimization supervisor for decentralized coordination of CAVs at unsignalized intersections. By dynamically tuning reward coefficients, the proposed approach mitigates instability and non-stationarity in multi-agent learning, achieving adaptive and scalable control under the CTDE paradigm. Beyond its application to traffic management, the framework provides a general perspective on integrating metaheuristic feedback into MARL systems to improve convergence, robustness, and causal interpretability. Future work will extend this architecture to mixed-traffic environments, investigate formal convergence guarantees, and explore hierarchical coordination across large-scale urban networks.

References

1. Abbas-Turki, A., et al.: Autonomous intersection management: optimal trajectories and efficient scheduling. Sensors **23**(3), 1509 (2023)
2. Antonio, G.P., Maria-Dolores, C.: Multi-agent deep reinforcement learning to manage connected autonomous vehicles at tomorrow's intersections. IEEE Trans. Veh. Technol. **71**(7), 7033–7043 (2022). https://doi.org/10.1109/TVT.2022.3169907
3. Antun, V., Renna, F., Poon, C., Adcock, B., Hansen, A.C.: On instabilities of deep learning in image reconstruction and the potential costs of AI. Proc. Natl. Acad. Sci. **117**(48), 30088–30095 (2020)
4. Carrasco, J., García, S., Rueda, M., Das, S., Herrera, F.: Recent trends in the use of statistical tests for comparing swarm and evolutionary computing algorithms: practical guidelines and a critical review. Swarm Evol. Comput. **54**, 100665 (2020)
5. Chouhan, A.P., Banda, G.: Autonomous intersection management: a heuristic approach. IEEE Access **6**, 53287–53295 (2018). https://doi.org/10.1109/ACCESS.2018.2871337

6. Deng, B., Sun, J., Li, Z., Wang, G.: Time-attenuating twin delayed DDPG reinforcement learning for trajectory tracking control of quadrotors (2023). https://doi.org/10.48550/arXiv.2302.06070
7. El-Qoraychy, F.Z., Dridi, M., Creput, J.C.: Deep reinforcement learning for vehicle intersection management in high-dimensional action spaces. In: Proceedings of the 2024 7th International Conference on Machine Learning and Machine Intelligence (MLMI), pp. 39–45. MLMI '24, Association for Computing Machinery, New York (2024). https://doi.org/10.1145/3696271.3696278
8. Garg, D., Chli, M., Vogiatzis, G.: Deep reinforcement learning for autonomous traffic light control. In: 2018 3rd IEEE International Conference on Intelligent Transportation Engineering (ICITE), pp. 214–218 (2018). https://doi.org/10.1109/ICITE.2018.8492537
9. Kalita, K., Ganesh, N., Balamurugan, S.: Metaheuristics for machine learning: algorithms and applications. John Wiley & Sons (2024)
10. Li, H., Dong, W., Lu, L., Wang, Y., Wang, X.: Distributed cooperative driving strategy for connected automated vehicles at unsignalized intersections based on monte carlo method. J. Adv. Transp. **2024**(1), 6586774 (2024)
11. Li, J., Dridi, M., El-Moudni, A.: A cooperative traffic control for the vehicles in the intersection based on the genetic algorithm. In: 2016 4th IEEE International Colloquium on Information Science and Technology (CiSt), pp. 627–632. IEEE (2016)
12. Mushtaq, A., ul Haq, I., Sarwar, M.A., Khan, A., Shafiq, O.: Traffic management of autonomous vehicles using policy based deep reinforcement learning and intelligent routing. arXiv:2206.14608 (2022)
13. Narayanan, R., Ganesh, N.: A comprehensive review of metaheuristics for hyperparameter optimization in machine learning, vol. 2, pp. 37–72. John Wiley & Sons, Ltd (2024). https://doi.org/10.1002/9781394233953.ch2, https://onlinelibrary.wiley.com/doi/abs/10.1002/9781394233953.ch2
14. Rios-Torres, J., Malikopoulos, A.A.: Automated and cooperative vehicle merging at highway on-ramps. IEEE Trans. Intell. Transp. Syst. **18**, 780–789 (2017). https://doi.org/10.1109/tits.2016.2587582
15. Seyyedabbasi, A., Aliyev, R., Kiani, F., Gulle, M.U., Basyildiz, H., Shah, M.A.: Hybrid algorithms based on combining reinforcement learning and metaheuristic methods to solve global optimization problems. Knowl.-Based Syst. **223**, 107044 (2021). https://doi.org/10.1016/j.knosys.2021.107044, https://www.sciencedirect.com/science/article/pii/S0950705121003075
16. Sun, K., Zhao, X., Wu, X.: A cooperative lane change model for connected and autonomous vehicles on two lanes highway by considering the traffic efficiency on both lanes. Transp. Res. Interdisciplinary Perspectives **9**, 100310 (2021). https://doi.org/10.1016/j.trip.2021.100310
17. Sun, Q., Zhang, L., Yu, H., Zhang, W., Mei, Y., Xiong, H.: Hierarchical reinforcement learning for dynamic autonomous vehicle navigation at intelligent intersections. In: Proceedings of the 29th ACM SIGKDD Conference on Knowledge Discovery and Data Mining, pp. 4852–4861 (2023). https://doi.org/10.1145/3580305.3599839
18. Talbi, E.G.: Machine learning into metaheuristics: a survey and taxonomy. ACM Comput. Surv. **54**(6) (2021). https://doi.org/10.1145/3459664
19. Talebpour, A., Mahmassani, H.S.: Influence of connected and autonomous vehicles on traffic flow stability and throughput. Transp. Res. Part C: Emerging Technol. **71**, 143–163 (2016). https://doi.org/10.1016/j.trc.2016.07.007, https://www.sciencedirect.com/science/article/pii/S0968090X16301140

20. Wu, Y., Zhu, F.: Junction management for connected and automated vehicles: intersection or roundabout? Sustainability **13**(16), 9482 (2021)
21. Xu, H., Cassandras, C.G., Li, L., Zhang, Y.: Comparison of cooperative driving strategies for cavs at signal-free intersections. IEEE Trans. Intell. Transp. Syst. **23**(7), 7614–7627 (2022). https://doi.org/10.1109/TITS.2021.3071456
22. Xu, Y., Zhou, H., Ma, T., Zhao, J., Qian, B., Shen, X.: Leveraging multiagent learning for automated vehicles scheduling at nonsignalized intersections. IEEE Internet Things J. **8**(14), 11427–11439 (2021). https://doi.org/10.1109/JIOT.2021.3054649
23. Yan, B., et al.: An algorithm framework for drug-induced liver injury prediction based on genetic algorithm and ensemble learning. Molecules **27**(10), 3112 (2022)
24. Yu, G., Li, H., Wang, Y., Chen, P., Zhou, B.: A review on cooperative perception and control supported infrastructure-vehicle system. Green Energy Intell. Transp. **1**(3), 100023 (2022). https://doi.org/10.1016/j.geits.2022.100023, https://www.sciencedirect.com/science/article/pii/S2773153722000238
25. Zhang, H., Du, Y., Zhao, S., Yuan, Y., Gao, Q.: VN-MADDPG: a variable-noise-based multi-agent reinforcement learning algorithm for autonomous vehicles at unsignalized intersections. Electronics **13**(16) (2024). https://www.mdpi.com/2079-9292/13/16/3180
26. Zhang, X., Zhou, Y., Huang, H., Luo, Q.: Enhanced salp search algorithm for optimization extreme learning machine and application to dew point temperature prediction. Int. J. Comput. Intell. Syst. **15**(1), 98 (2022)
27. Zhao, R., Li, Y., Gao, F., Gao, Z., Zhang, T.: Multi-agent constrained policy optimization for conflict-free management of connected autonomous vehicles at unsignalized intersections. IEEE Trans. Intell. Transp. Syst. **25**(6), 5374–5388 (2024). https://doi.org/10.1109/TITS.2023.3331723

Author Index

If you have any questions about our products, please contact us on:
ProductSafety.EU@springernature.com

Springer Nature Customer Service Center GmbH
Tiergartenstr. 3, 69121 Heidelberg, Germany

FSC
MIX
FSC C103264